The Complete
IDIOT'S
Pocket
Guide to
MS-DOS 6.2

by Kelly Oliver

GW00806367

alpha
books

A Division of Prentice Hall Computer Publishing
201 West 103rd Street, Indianapolis, IN 46290 USA

International Standard Book Number:1-56761-417-5
Library of Congress Catalog Card Number: 93-73522

95 94   9 8 7 6 5 4 3

Interpretation of the printing code: the rightmost number of the first series of numbers is the year of the book's printing; the rightmost number of the second series of numbers is the number of the book's printing. For example, a printing code of 93-1 shows that the first printing of the book occurred in 1993.

Screen reproductions in this book were created by means of the program Collage Plus from Inner Media, Inc., Hollis, NH.

Printed in the United States of America

Publisher, Marie Butler-Knight; **Associate Publisher**, Lisa A. Bucki; **Managing Editor**, Elizabeth Keaffaber; **Development Editor**, Seta Frantz; **Manuscript Editor**, San Dee Phillips; **Cover Designer**, Scott Fullmer; **Designer**, Roger Morgan; **Indexer**, Jeanne Clark; **Production Team**; Gary Adair, Diana Bigham, Katy Bodenmiller, Brad Chinn, Tim Cox, Meshell Dinn, Mark Enochs, Beth Rago, Marc Shecter, Greg Simsic

Special thanks to C. Herbert Feltner for ensuring the technical accuracy of this book.

Contents

Introduction

Your Computer Won't Work Without It

MS-DOS: The Captain of Your Computer

Say you're taking a trip. You will get in a car, hop on a plane, jump on a ship, whatever. No matter what mode of transportation you choose, there will always be a single person in charge of getting you where you want to go. In a car, it's the driver. In a plane, it's the pilot. On a boat, it's the captain. You get the picture.

MS-DOS is like the captain of your computer. (*DOS* stands for disk operating system, which means that it controls how your computer interprets the commands you give it.) You tell it where you want to go and what you want to do, and DOS takes you there. If you want to copy a file, you type in the COPY command and DOS copies the file. Very little work is required on your part. All you have to do is make sure that you give DOS the right instructions. You could wind up in your own little proverbial Bermuda Triangle if you aren't careful.

Thus enters this book. If you follow along carefully, you'll learn how to give DOS the right instructions and everything will turn out peachy. You'll soon be able to do all sorts of things with DOS. You'll put a quick end to the dreaded **Bad command or file name** error messages that seem to crop up all the time.

How to Use This Book

The Complete Idiot's Pocket Guide to MS-DOS 6.2 is designed to be a friendly, easy-to-use manual for those of us who are short of time but who need to know the basics about using DOS. Each lesson is brief and to the point, and is written with a conversational tone so you won't feel like you have to read each sentence twelve times to understand it.

There are special, little features like tips and figures that will help you along the way. You can look at the figures to see examples of the way your screen should look when you perform certain commands or follow a set of instructions.

The tips look like this:

Read This! If you read one of these babies, you'll find some information that might turn out to be pretty handy.

Use the following conventions to help you work through lessons:

On-screen text	Text that appears on-screen appears in **bold**.
Menu, dialog box, and window name	The first letter of each menu, dialog box or window name is capitalized.
What you type	The information you type is **bold**.
What you press	The keys you press (for key combinations or commands) appear in **bold**.
Selection letters	The selection letter of each command or option is **bold** (such as **F**ile).

You can read the lessons in this book from start to finish, or you can skip around from lesson to lesson. Use this book however you feel most comfortable.

Acknowledgments

I'd like to thank the author of *10 Minute Guide to DOS 6.2*, Jennifer Fulton, for sharing her DOS expertise with me. Special thanks go to my extraordinary editors and direction-givers: Seta Frantz and San Dee Phillips.

Dedication

For Kyle Passon—"It's just the way I smile."

Lesson 1

What Is This DOS Thing?

Let's Start 'Er Up!

First things first. Before you can start learning about DOS, you have to start your PC so you'll have a way to practice what you learn. The process of starting a computer is called *booting*. When your PC boots, the disk operating system (DOS) is copied (*loaded*) into memory. *Memory* is the working area of your PC, where the computer temporarily stores information it needs. Did you catch all that?

You can load DOS from a *hard disk* or from a *diskette*. (Your hard disk is permanently stored in your computer and is usually drive C. A diskette is a portable floppy disk that you can insert and remove from a floppy disk drive.) If you've already installed DOS on your hard disk, you just have to turn on your computer. Find the computer's ON switch and flip it, and turn on the monitor. That's it!

If your PC doesn't have a hard disk or doesn't have DOS installed yet, put the *system disk* in drive A, and turn on the computer. The system disk is the MS-DOS 6.2 Setup Disk 1 Diskette. When you boot this way, DOS is copied from the diskette into memory.

Always Be Prepared   Like a good scout, you should always be prepared for emergencies. That's why you should always make copies of your installation disks (especially if you use them to start your computer every day). If you don't know how to make copies, skip ahead to Lesson 11 for more information.

Once your PC is started, it may ask you for the current date and time, like a passerby on the street. (If your PC has an internal clock, as most do, you may not see these prompts.) DOS uses the time and date every time you save a file. It may seem insignificant now, but you'll realize how important the correct time and date are if you have four versions of one document but you only want the one you looked at last Friday. If you see the prompt:

Current date is 01-01-80
Enter new date:

then enter the current date (after the colon) in one of three formats. For example:

02-20-93

02/20/93

02.20.93

If you see the prompt:

Current time is 00:00:01
Enter new time:

then enter the current time (after the colon) using 24-hour military time. (Apparently, all computers served in the armed forces.) For example, to enter 2:12 p.m., type **14:12** and press **Enter**. You may also enter the seconds, as in **14:12:33**.

I Started My PC, Now Tell Me What DOS Is

DOS stands for *disk operating system*, which means it's the thing that's responsible for the operation of your computer. Did you think you were responsible for your computer's operation? Well, not really. You could type till the cows come home, but commands don't make any sense to your computer unless it has an operating system to tell it how to interpret the commands you are typing. See how it works?

For example, a program may tell DOS to read the contents of a file, and DOS takes care of the details. (You'll learn more about files in Lesson 2.) DOS carries out all your commands and does all the horrid detail work so you don't have to. How handy.

DOS provides two ways for you to give it instructions: the *DOS command line* and the *DOS Shell*. When you use the DOS command line, you enter a string of characters at the *DOS prompt*. The DOS prompt looks something like **C>** or **C:\>**.

To enter a DOS command, you type the command after the DOS prompt. You enter the command after the greater-than sign (>), as shown in Figure 1.1. After you type the command, you have to press the **Enter** key to make DOS aware that you've typed something. For example, type **MEM**, and then hit **Enter** to make DOS report how much available memory it has.

DOS command

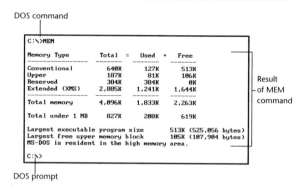

```
C:\>MEM

Memory Type      Total =    Used +   Free
-----------      -----      ----     ----
Conventional     640K       127K     513K
Upper            187K        81K     106K
Reserved         384K       384K       0K
Extended (XMS)  2,885K     1,241K   1,644K
                 ------     ------   ------
Total memory    4,096K     1,833K   2,263K

Total under 1 MB 827K       208K     619K

Largest executable program size       513K (525,056 bytes)
Largest free upper memory block       105K (107,904 bytes)
MS-DOS is resident in the high memory area.

C:\>
```

Result of MEM command

DOS prompt

Figure 1.1 *Entering commands at the DOS prompt.*

The Mysterious AUTOEXEC.BAT and the Elusive CONFIG.SYS

If you hang around computer geeks, you've undoubt-edly heard them tossing around strange-sounding words like "otto eggzek bat" and "kunfig sis." No? Then you've been hanging around posers. Those people aren't real computer geeks, they're faking it.

Those strange-sounding words, translated into com-puterese, are really two very important DOS files: AUTOEXEC.BAT and CONFIG.SYS. If you want to really get to know your computer, get to know these files. AUTOEXEC.BAT and CONFIG.SYS are DOS's startup files, which means that you can put stuff in these files to tell DOS what you want it to do when it starts your computer. Geeks call that *configuration*.

When I first started using DOS, no one told me what these files were. All I knew was that I should never, ever touch or change these files or I would probably break my computer. (Which, by the way, is hooey. It is very hard to break a computer. However, it is true that you shouldn't edit your startup files without making backup copies first.)

So Quit Stalling and Tell Me What AUOTEXEC.BAT Is

First of all, AUTOEXEC.BAT is a *batch* file (which accounts for the .BAT extension) that DOS 6.2 creates when you install it. Batch files are simply files that contain lists of DOS commands. When you run the batch file, DOS executes all the commands in the file one at a time. This is really handy because you can type one command to run the batch file instead of typing twenty or so commands one by one.

What's a File? If you're really new to DOS, you might be confused with all this talk of files. Go ahead and skip to Lesson 2 and read all about files and such things. When you're done, flip back to this lesson. I'll just wait here for you.

This particular batch file is *AUTO*matically *EXEC*uted when you boot your computer. It contains very useful things like your *path statement* (more on that in Lesson 3) and your *prompt* information (more in Lesson 3, as well).

In addition to the commands placed in the AUTOEXEC.BAT by the DOS 6.2 installation program, you can add your own commands to be executed at startup. For example, you could place a command in the AUTOEXEC.BAT to automatically start some other program for you. Moreover, you can press the F8 key when you start your PC, and select which commands you want executed, skipping over the commands you don't want to use right now. I'll be telling you more about nifty AUTOEXEC.BAT things in future lessons, so keep your eyes peeled.

What's the Other One Good For?

Fortunately, you usually don't have to worry about CONFIG.SYS; it can generally take care of itself. As with the AUTOEXEC.BAT file, the DOS 6.2 installation program creates the CONFIG.SYS file for you and places certain commands in it automatically. It's basically just used to customize DOS.

For example, there's a line in your CONFIG.SYS file that says **FILES=** followed by some number. That number is the default amount of files you can have open at one time. Now, say you have a certain program that requires a tremendous amount of files to be open at once. You will have to change the FILES line in your CONFIG.SYS file so that the right amount of files can be opened.

How Do I Change My File?   You'll learn how to edit your files in Lesson 19. You don't have to worry about it right now, just keep in mind that you can change the file to set your own defaults. That's the key.

Like the AUTOEXEC.BAT file, you can select which commands are executed within the CONFIG.SYS at start-up. This enables you to fine-tune your PC for the programs you'll be using throughout each day. I'll be telling you more about this file in future lessons, so consider yourself warned.

Feel like you've been overwhelmed with DOS information? This is only the beginning! Get ready to learn more about disks, directories, and files in the next lesson. Sounds like a hoot!

Lesson 2

The Three D's: Disks, Directories, and de Files

Let's Start with Disks

As I mentioned in the last lesson, your computer uses two types of disks: *hard disks* and *floppy disks*. Hard disks are for permanent storage of files and programs. Floppy disks (often called simply *diskettes*), are for portable (removable) storage.

Under your computer's proverbial hood is a hard disk (usually drive C). It is used to store your programs, documents, and DOS. You can copy these files onto diskettes, where they serve as backups in case the hard disk gets damaged in some way.

Diskettes are small plastic squares with magnetic disks in them. They come in two sizes: 5 1/4-inches and 3 1/2-inches, as shown in Figure 2.1. Each size diskette comes in *high-density* and *double-density* versions. (In addition, 3 1/2-inch diskettes also come in an extended-density version, but we won't worry about that particular one because you probably won't be using it.)

Maybe I'm Dense, But Just What Does Density Mean? *Density* describes the amount of information the diskette can hold. High-density diskettes hold at least twice as much information as the same size double-density diskettes because the information on high-density diskettes is packed closer together.

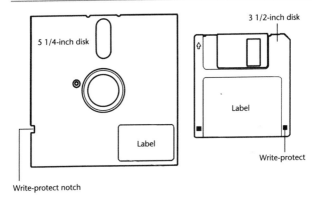

Figure 2.1 *Diskettes come in two sizes.*

The Destiny of Your Density Buy diskettes that match the type of diskette drive your computer uses. This means you have to buy not only the right size diskette (5 1/4-inch or 3 1/2-inch), *but also the right density.* You can use double-density disks in a high-density drive, but you can't use high-density disks at all unless you have a high-density drive. Yikes, this is getting really dense!

To keep all this mumbo-jumbo straight, disks are assigned letters. Your computer's first diskette drive is called A, and a second drive is called B. Your computer's hard disk is called C, and additional hard disks are called D, E, and so on.

Disks are represented by their drive letter followed by a colon, as in C: and A:. That means that when you want to switch drives, you type the drive letter you want and a colon, and then press **Enter**.

What Are Files?

Hard disks and diskettes are used to store your *data*. (Computer geeks say "data" because it sounds more technical than "stuff" or "grocery list.") You save your data in files, which are like tiny file folders. You store different kinds of data in different files. Each file has its own special name.

A long time ago, the DOS masters decided that file names can have up to eight *characters* (letters or numbers) and a three digit *extension*, which helps to identify the contents or purpose of the file. For example, if you named a file BALLYHOO.DOC, the extension .DOC would identify the file as a document file. Get it?

What Are You Going to Name It?

The names of files must follow certain conventions. Here's a handy list of valid *characters*:

- ☞ Any letter, from A to Z.

- ☞ Any single digit number, from 0 to 9.

- ☞ One of these special characters: $ # & @ ! % ( ) - { } ' _ ` ^ ~

Here's a list of other restrictions and limitations:

- ☞ Uppercase is the same as lowercase. For example, the file name WORK.DOC is the same as work.doc.

- ☞ No spaces, commas, or backslashes are allowed in file names.

- ☞ Use a period only to separate the file name from the extension, as in BALLYHOO.DOC. You cannot include a period as part of the file name. For example, 93.OCT.DOC is *not* a valid file name.

Congratulations, It's a Directory

Because you can have thousands of files on your computer, you store them in directories so you know where they are. Directories help you stay organized. They're like trees. There's a root directory (usually drive C), then other directories branching out from it, and then subdirectories branching out from those directories.

Let's examine our DOS tree. The root directory is represented by a single backslash (\), so the root directory of drive C is **C:**. Only general-purpose files (such as the CONFIG.SYS and AUTOEXEC.BAT files) should be placed in the root directory.

Branching out from the root directory, you create other directories, one for each program you use. Try a different analogy: a hallway. If you think of these directories as rooms, you could have a room for Budget, Sales, Marketing, and so on, as shown in figure 2.2.

Figure 2.2 *Organize your files in directories and subdirectories.*

You can separate the files you create (documents) from the program files (created by someone else) by creating *subdirectories*. To continue our room analogy, you could think of subdirectories as closets within each room. Directories are represented by a backslash, followed by the name of the directory, as in **C:\SALES**. Subdirectories are separated from their parent directory by another backslash, as in **C:\SALES\JOE**.

Have You Chosen A Name Yet? You have to follow the same rules and regulations when creating directory names as you did when you created file names. (By the way, you'll learn how to create directories in Lesson **9**.) However, most users do not use an extension when naming a directory. You can, if you want, but no cool people use extensions in directories. That makes it hard to tell the difference between files and directories.

How Do I Switch to a Different Directory?

Because each *program* (application) you own is placed in its own directory, you change directories as you switch from program to program. By changing directories, you can access the program's files more easily.

To change directories, use the CD command (CD stands for **c**hange **d**irectory). Simply type **CD** and then a backslash (\), followed by the name of the directory you want to go to. For example, to change to the DOS directory, type:

CD\DOS

Yow! What Went Wrong? Be careful to type a backslash (\) and not a forward slash (/) when entering the CD command.

Sometimes, you'll create *subdirectories* (directories within other directories). For example, earlier we saw a subdirectory called JOE in a directory called SALES. To change to the JOE directory, you have to go through the SALES directory. We would use the command:

CD\SALES\JOE

Did you notice how an additional backslash (\) separates the directory names? To change to the root directory, type this:

CD

Now that you're all bogged down with lots of details about disks, files, and directories, let's learn some DOS basics. (It won't all be this excruciatingly boring, I promise.)

Lesson 3

Shuffling Around in DOS

DOS Prompt-o-Rama

The DOS prompt is the on-screen marker that beckons you to enter a command. When you type a command, it appears after the prompt. The DOS prompt normally looks like this: **C>**. However, since this type of prompt is not very informative, many people change the DOS prompt so that it shows the current drive and directory. This is what that looks like: **C:\DOS>**. Commands you type appear after your DOS prompt.

All Right Then, Show Me How to Change It

As you move from program to program, changing directories, it's easy to get lost and forget which directory you're in. I should know, I've done it hundreds of times. Why should you care which directory you're in? Well, DOS commands act on files in the current directory. For example, if you had no idea what directory you were in and you went around deleting a bunch of files, you could accidently delete files in the *wrong directory*. Very bad news, indeed.

You can customize the DOS prompt so it displays the current directory, the current time, and other things. So instead of the rather boring DOS prompt, you can change it to something really exciting, like:

C:\DOS>

14:32 C:\DOS>

Tues 09-21-1993>

There are lots of things that you can do with the DOS prompt to customize it to suit your needs. To change your DOS prompt, you use the PROMPT command. For example, to display the current drive and directory (**C:\WORD>**), type this: **PROMPT PG**.

To display the date, include **$D** with the PROMPT command. To include the time, use **$T**. If you ever want to get back to the default DOS prompt, just type **PROMPT** and press **Enter**. That's it.

This Is All Very Interesting, But How Do I Use DOS?

Entering a DOS command is easy. You just type the command and press **Enter**. Wah-lah. For example, to get the current date, type **DATE** and press **Enter**. You can type DOS commands in upper- or lowercase. For example, the command **DATE** is the same as **date**. DOS doesn't care.

A DOS command is made up of three very important parts:

- ☞ **The command itself** For example, the **DIR** command, which is used to list the files in a directory. (You'll learn more about DIR in Lesson 6. I bet you can't wait.)

- ☞ **Applicable parameters** *Parameters* tell DOS which files, directories, or drives with which to work. For example, you can type **DIR HOOEY.DOC** to list a specific file. HOOEY.DOC is the parameter.

- ☞ **Applicable switches** *Switches* are options you can use with a command. Switches are almost always preceded with a forward slash (/). (This is different from the backslash thingy.) For example, the DIR command has a switch (/P for page) that tells DOS to list the files one page at a time. That way, you can see all your files instead of just watching them scroll by at an annoyingly rapid pace.

Between each part of a DOS command, you must insert a space. For example, the command **DIR *.DOC /P** includes a single space between the *command* **DIR**, the *parameter* ***.DOC**, and the *command switch* /**P**. So, although it may be hard to see the spaces in this book, always remember to type a space after each DOS command, and any other part of the command.

Rats! I've Messed It Up Already

If you type a mistake *before you press Enter*, try one of these easy cures:

- ☛ **Press the Backspace key**   Back up and erase the incorrect characters and retype them.
- ☛ **Insert or delete characters**   Move the blinking cursor to the place where you want to insert a character by using the arrow keys. Once you have the cursor positioned, press any character, and it will be inserted at that spot. To delete an extra character, press **Delete** or **Del**.
- ☛ **Press the Esc key**   This will erase the entire line and let you start over.

If you've pressed **Enter** but got one of those irritating error messages because you mistyped the command, repeat the command by pressing **F3**. Then use the arrow keys to position the cursor where you'd like to insert or delete characters.

To stop a command in progress, hold down the **Ctrl** key while pressing the **Break** key. If you can't find the **Break** key, use **Ctrl+C** instead.

What's That Little Arrow Thingy? Pressing the **Ctrl** key produces the character, ^. So, if you press **Ctrl+C**, you will see ^**C** on your monitor. See how it works?

External and Internal Commands

Okay, there's one kind of kooky thing you should know about DOS: it has *internal* and *external* commands. The internal ones are loaded into memory at startup, and you never have to worry about them. It's those external ones that you have to worry about.

External DOS commands are stored in the DOS directory. That means that when you want to use them, you have to be in the DOS directory. (I warned you about the importance of being in the proper directory earlier, remember?) You see, DOS won't know what the command is unless it can find it. You have to tell DOS which directory it needs to look in to find the command. To do that, you could add a *path* in front of an external command, like this:

C:\DOS\FORMAT A:

But that's downright confusing. To give DOS access to *all* the commands (both internal and external)— regardless of what directory you're currently in—you should create a permanent path. To do this, include the following command in your AUTOEXEC.BAT file (flip to Lesson 19 for instructions on how to edit your AUTOEXEC.BAT):

PATH=C:\DOS

The **PATH** command tells DOS to look for its external commands in the \DOS directory, so you don't have to worry about which directory you're in when you enter a command. With this PATH statement in your AUTOEXEC.BAT, you could enter just the command, and DOS would know what you mean.

Paths to Other Places You can (and should) include other directories in the PATH statement too, so that you can start your programs from any directory. (PATH finds only program files, not data files.) Just separate the directory names by semicolons. Put the directories you use the most at the front of your path.

You're ready to go. You know all about the DOS prompt, and you know how to enter a command and set up your path statement. Now it's time to show you some tricks for entering DOS commands. Entering commands is as easy as pulling a rabbit out of a hat.

Lesson 4

For My Next Trick, Entering Commands

The Old Path Editing Gag

In the last lesson, we talked about changing directories and having the right path to the file you want. To refresh your memory, let's go over paths one more time. The *path* for a file consists of its:

Drive   A drive designation is made up of the drive letter, followed by a colon (which indicates that you are talking about a disk drive). For example, if a file is located on drive C, then **C:** would be the first part of that file's path.

Directory path   A directory path is made up of a backslash (\) followed by the name of the directory, followed by another backslash. A subdirectory is indicated by entering the name of the subdirectory, followed by another backslash. For example, if you had a file in a directory called PIGGY, which is a subdirectory of WORD, the directory path would be **\WORD\PIGGY**.

File name   This part is easy—it's the name of the file, as in **OINK.DOC**.

The completed path in the above example would look like this: **C:\WORD\PIGGY\OINK.DOC**. When entering commands, be sure to get the path right. Otherwise, poor DOS will get confused.

> **Tip**
>
> **Oh, My Tired Fingers!**   Don't use the complete path for a file name unless you have to. If the file you are trying to use is located in the current directory, just type the file name, and DOS will know what you mean.

Amazing Wild-Card Tricks

To specify a group of files to be used with a command, use *wild cards*. For example, you might type the command **DEL *.*** to delete all the files in the current directory.(More on the DEL command in Lesson 8.) DOS provides two wild cards for specifying commands:

- ☞ The **asterisk (*)** represents several consecutive characters in a file name.
- ☞ The **question mark (?)** represents a single character within a file name.

Here are some examples: If you want to specify all files that end in .DOC, you would type ***.DOC**. If you want to specify all files that begin with **BUDGET** (such as BUDGET92.WKS, BUDGET93.WKS, and BUDGET93.CHT), type **BUDGET*.***. If you want to specify all the files in a directory, use ***.***.

If you know you want to leave room only for a single character, you would use the question mark wild card. For example, to specify the files CHAP1.DOC through CHAP9.DOC (but not CHAP10.DOC), type **CHAP?.DOC**. This really isn't hard once you get the hang of it.

Syntax: Bunch of Hooey or Important Concept?

Remember what *parameters* are from the last lesson? They tell DOS what file or other object to act upon. For example, the DEL command is used to delete a file. You obviously have to tell DOS which files you want to delete, so the parameter you use with the DEL command is the name of the file you want deleted. The command looks like this: **DEL DUMBFILE.DOC**.

We also discussed *switches* in the last lesson. They are the little options that you enter after the command. For example, to see what programs are in memory, you enter **MEM /C**. You can use as many switches as you want—for example, to display the programs in memory, one screenful at a time, you enter **MEM /C /P**.

To summarize briefly, DOS commands consist of several elements:

- ☞ *The command itself,* for example, **FORMAT**.

- ☞ *Optional parameters* which explain what drives or files to act on, for example, **A:**.

- ☞ *Optional switches* which allow a single command to act in a variety of ways,   for example, /F:360.

The completed command could look like this: **FORMAT A: /F:360**.

So what's syntax, then? Well, it's the order that you type the stuff in. The command always goes first, then parameters, then switches. If you have any trouble figuring out the command's syntax, look in on-line help. (See Lesson 5 for more on the help sytem.) It'll show you how the command is supposed to be typed.

A sample command syntax could look like this:

DEL [*d:*][*path*]*filename.ext*

The stuff in brackets is optional. You don't have to use it unless you need to. The italicized words are placeholders; you just substitute the real name for what you want.

I Still Don't Get It   If you're having problems getting a command right, you can turn to Appendix B, which contains a DOS command syntax reference.

Consider yourself armed with all the basic DOS knowledge you need to know. Before you jump right in, however, take a look at the next lesson, which tells you how to get help when you need it.

Lesson 5

Help Wanted!

Won't You Please, Please Help Me?

Say you're trying to enter a DOS command and you can't figure out how it's supposed to be typed. Every time you press **Enter**, you get the blasted **Bad command or file name** error message. Before you go completely bonkers, try using the on-line help system. It can do wonders for you.

Whenever you need help with a certain command, you can type the command followed by /?, like this: **DIR /?**

You'll see a description of what the command does, folllowed by a whole bunch of gobbledegook, like this:

> **Displays a list of files and subdirectories in a directory.**
>
> **DIR [drive:][path][filename] [/P] [/W] [/A[[:]attribs]] [/O[[:]sortord]] [/S] [/B] [/L] [/C[H]]**

That last line is the syntax I talked about in Lesson 4. It tells you what order you're supposed to type everything in. If you're still confused, go for the gusto and access the DOS help system.

You Call This Help?

I know, the syntax line like the one shown above isn't always very helpful. It doesn't really mean much unless you know what all the switch letters stand for. If you really need help and not just a little hint, go straight to the DOS help system. How, you ask? Easy. Type the word **HELP** and press **Enter**. Did you think there was a trick to it or something?

When you get into the help system, you'll see a list of commands. Use the arrow keys to select one, and then press **Enter**.

Specific Help To go directly to a particular command, type it after the word **HELP**, as in: **HELP DIR**.

After you select the command you want, you'll see a listing of the syntax and the parameters for a command, as shown in Figure 5.1. Press **Page Down** to see more (press **Page Up** to go back).

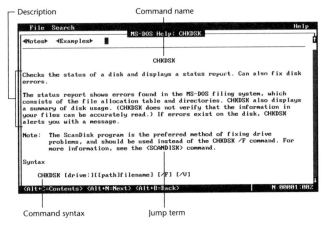

Figure 5.1   The DOS help system in all its glory.

If you see a word in angle brackets, such as **<Tree>**, it's a *jump* term. Press **Tab** until the cursor moves to a jump term, then press **Enter** to select it. You will jump to another section of the help system that contains information about the jump term. (Hence the word "jump.") If you use a mouse, you can also *click* (press the left mouse button) on a jump term to select it.

Quick Jump   You can jump forward, backward, or straight to the table of contents by pressing **Alt+N**, **Alt+B**, or **Alt+C**. Those are called *key combinations,* and when you see one, it means to hold down the first key (in this case, **Alt**) and then press the second key. Release both keys at the same time.

At the top of the first screen for each command, you will see the words **Notes** and **Examples**. Under **Notes**, you'll find additional tips and cautions about using the command. **Examples** lists several ways to type the command, as shown in Figure 5.2. Use the **Tab** key until the cursor moves to either of these items, and press **Enter** to select them. If you use a mouse, you can click on either one to select it.

To return to the syntax screen, select **Syntax**.

Searching for That Special Something

Want to go to a particular command? I know you do. First, you open the Search *menu* by clicking on it or by pressing **Alt+S**. Then, select the Find command by clicking on it or by pressing **F**. Type the name of the command you're looking for, such as **DIR**, and then press **Enter**.

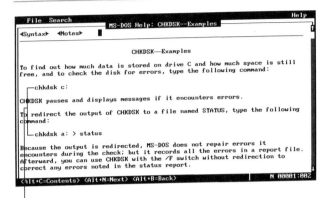

Example

Figure 5.2 *The DOS help system includes examples for each command. Lucky you.*

What's a Menu?   Across the top of the help screen is the menu bar. It lists the menus that are available. Menus are basically just categories of similar commands.

I Wish I Had This on Paper

If you use particular commands quite often, you may want to print out parts of the DOS help system for easy access. In fact, it's probably a good idea. If you want to print something, first move to the section of the DOS help system you want to print. Then, open the File menu by pressing **Alt+F** or by clicking on it with the mouse. With the menu open, select the **Print** command by pressing **P** or by clicking on it. Shazam! Your very own copy, all printed out on nice paper for you.

Get Me Outta Here!

To exit the help system and return to a DOS prompt, press **Alt+F** to open the File menu. Press **X** to select Exit. You can't get any easier than that.

Hopefully, you'll never again have any trouble with DOS because now you know where to turn when you need help. In the next lesson, you'll learn how to list your files so you can see what you've got in certain disks and directories.

Lesson 6

Listing Files with DIR

List-Makers of the World, Unite!

Are you the type of person who makes lots of lists? I am. I make errands lists, grocery lists, goals lists—I've got a list for everything under the sun. Lists are handy for finding out what you have and what you don't have, where you've been and where you're going.

With DOS, you can make lists of all your files so you can see what you've got. Using the DIR command to list the files in a directory is like reading the table of contents for a book—it's a great way to become familiar with your PC and find out what's on it. Or if you've ever had the frustrating experience of misplacing a file that you were working on just moments ago, the DIR command can help you find it.

The DIR command consists of three basic parts, two of which are optional. First, you type the command (DIR). Then, you can optionally specify the path name (the drive, directory, and file name), then any switches you might want to use.

The complete syntax for the DIR command is listed in Appendix B. For now, let's start with the basics. To list the files in the current directory, type: **DIR /P** and press **Enter**. You see something like Figure 6.1. The /P switch tells DOS to stop the file listing when it fills a page. To continue with the listing, just press **Enter**.

Whoa, Nellie! You should always include the **/P** switch with the DIR command, especially if you've got tons of files like I do. The little suckers will zip right by before you get a chance to see what they are. If you want, you can customize the DIR command so that it always includes /P. Add this command to your AUTOEXEC.BAT (see Lesson 19 for instructions on editing files): **SET DIRCMD=/P**. From then on, every time you type **DIR**, DOS will automatically interpret it as if you had typed the /P switch.

Wide Load You can display files across the screen (instead of down) by including the **/W** switch, as in **DIR /W**. However, the file information will not be displayed.

DIR lists additional information about each file, besides its name. For example, the size of each file is listed in *bytes*.

What the Heck Is a Byte, Anyway? The smallest unit of measurement of computer data, equal to one character, such as the letter J or the number 8. Larger data amounts are measured in *kilobytes* or *megabytes*. (A kilobyte is roughly one thousand bytes, a megabyte is roughly one million.)

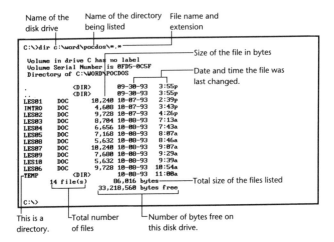

Figure 6.1   Listing the files in a directory. Pretty nifty, eh?

But I Want to Use a Different Drive

You're not limited to just the C: drive. You can list files from whichever drive you want. When you're "talking" to DOS through the command prompt, it assumes that the current drive and directory is the "subject" of your conversation. That's why you get a listing of the files in the root directory of your hard disk when you type **DIR** at the **C:\>** prompt.

To list the files on another drive, you could change to that drive (as you learned in Lesson 2), and then type **DIR**. But the simplest way to list files on another drive (such as a diskette) is to include the drive letter with the DIR command, like this: **DIR A: /P**.

Because you specified drive A, the files on drive A will be listed instead of those on drive C. This saves you the trouble of switching between drives. Not that it's a lot of trouble or anything, but it might save you a few seconds. Maybe you're really pressed for time.

How Do I Use a Different Directory?

By default, DIR lists files in the *current directory* only. To see the contents of a different directory, you must either make the desired directory active by changing to that directory (as you learned in Lesson 2), and then type **DIR**, or you must specify the directory name with the DIR command.

You can get dizzy changing directories all the time, so the easiest way to list files in another directory is to include the directory name with the DIR command. For example, if you wanted to list the files in the WORD directory without leaving the directory you're in, you would type: **DIR \WORD /P**. Even though you might be in a different directory, the files in the WORD directory would be listed instead. It's like seeing into the next room without actually going into that room. Kind of.

List It Your Way

Looking for a particular order for your files? They are normally displayed in the order in which they are stored on disk, but you can force DOS to display the files in some kind of reasonable order, such as *alphabetically*. Type this: **DIR /O /P**.

This command lists subdirectories first, then files, sorted by file name. How clever! You can sort files in other ways; see DOS help for more information.

I'm Picky; I Only Want Certain Files

If you're looking for a particular file, or a particular file type (extension), you can use *wild cards* to list selected files. You learned about wild cards in Lesson 4, but as a quick review:

- ☛ **The asterisk (*)** represents several characters within a file name.
- ☛ **The question mark (?)** is used to represent a single character within a file name.

To list selected files, simply type **DIR** followed by the file name pattern, like this: **DIR JUNK??.* /P**.

This command lists (one screenful at a time) all the files in the current directory that start with the letters JUNK, followed by two characters, and any extension.

The File Lost and Found

If you've ever had the experience of saving a file, only to lose it when you need to use it again, this variation of the DIR command will come in handy. You can use this command to locate a file anywhere on your hard disk. For example, to find the file LOST.DOC, you would type:

DIR C:\LOST.DOC /S

The /S switch tells DIR to look in the current directory, and all subdirectories. By adding C:\ in front of the file name, DIR does not start its search in the current directory, but in the root directory.

Let's Print This Baby!

When you use the DIR command (or any other command, for that matter), the result of that command is displayed on the monitor. You can redirect the output to a different device, such as your printer. Why would you want to do this? Well, sometimes it's easier to flip pages than to scan through a directory listing on-screen. Actually, I think it's *usually* easier to do that. Also, it's easier to organize diskettes if you have a printout of their contents. To send a listing of all the files on a diskette in drive A to the printer, use this command:

DIR A: /W >PRN

The greater-than sign (>) is the *redirection symbol*; PRN is DOS's name for your printer. Since you'll probably only want to print the file names (and not the other DIR information), I included the /W switch.

You can also redirect the info to another file, so you can save it permanently or print it out later. To save a listing of the current directory in a file, use a command like this:

DIR >FILE.LST

Well, are you getting sick of DOS yet? I hope not, because this is just the beginning. Next, you'll learn how to copy and move files. Now we're getting into the real nitty-gritty.

Lesson 7

Duplicating and Relocating

A Word to the Wise

There's a difference between copying and moving files, in case you didn't know. When you copy a file, you end up with two files: the copy and the original. When you move a file, you still have only one file—it's just been moved to a different directory on your disk.

I find myself doing a lot of copying and moving. In fact, these could be two of the most common commands you'll use. With the COPY command, you can easily make copies of important files and store them on diskettes for safe-keeping. Should something happen to your PC's hard disk, you'd still have your original files (the programs you could reload from their original diskettes).

If you wanted to print a document on another PC, you could use the COPY command to place a copy of the document on diskette, and then you could use the COPY command again to copy the document from that diskette to the other PC's hard disk (or you could just print it from the diskette). See? Endless possibilities.

The MOVE command allows you to reorganize your documents so you can find them easily. For example, you could decide to create a subdirectory halfway through a project for all the files related to it. After creating the subdirectory (which you'll learn how to do in Lesson 9), you could move the files from their current directory to their private one. Very handy.

Cloning 101: Copying Files

The COPY command consists of three basic parts. First, the name of the command (COPY), the file to copy, and then the directory where you want the duplicate to go. You don't *have* to specify where to copy the files, but if you don't, DOS will copy them to the current directory or drive.

> **Don't Be Such a Copy Cat!**   DOS 6.2 will prompt you if you attempt to copy a file on top of an existing copy of the same file. For example, if you copy the file HOLYCOW.DOC from a diskette into your \WORD directory and a HOLYCOW.DOC file already exists there, you'll be prompted. Press **Y** to overlay the file, or **N** to abort the copy process.

For example, suppose you wanted to copy your budget file onto a diskette in drive A for safekeeping. You would type **COPY BUDGET.DOC A:** and press **Enter**. If you get the message **File not found**, DOS was unable to find the BUDGET.DOC file (you could have misspelled the file name, but the error is more likely because you are not in the directory where the file is kept). In that case, change to the directory where the file is located, and then type the COPY command again.

Or if you prefer a one-step operation, include the file path with the COPY command, like this:

COPY C:\123\BUDGET.WKS A:

Personally, I hate copying files that way. I think it's a pain in the neck. I always switch directories first. But you can do it however you want.

I Don't Want to Copy It, I Just Want to Give It a New Name

If you just want to change the name of a file, use the **REN** command. It's a different animal altogether. The format of the REN (rename) command is simple: **REN *originalname newname***. For example, to rename your budget file to reflect the current year, type:

REN BUDGET.WKS BUDGET93.WKS

When renaming files, remember all the naming rules and regulations that I outlined in Lesson 2. Also, don't change the extension of the file unless you know exactly what you're doing. (In our example, we kept the .WKS extension the same on the renamed file.) Programs use these extensions to identify their files and their purpose, and if files are not named correctly, your program may not be able to use them.

Variations on a Theme

The COPY command is very versatile; you can use it to copy files from one directory to another, from your hard disk to a diskette, or from a diskette to your hard disk. Unfortunately, its versatility is what also makes the COPY command a bit difficult.

I've generously compiled a big, long list of samples of common COPY situations. Use these as guides whenever you use the COPY command:

☛ **Copying files to a different directory.** Suppose you wanted to copy all your letters from the \WORD directory to a new directory called \LETTERS. (This will create copies of the files in two places; if you want to move files, see the last section in this lesson.) Type these commands:

CD\WORD

COPY *.LTR C:\LETTERS

To accomplish this in one step, use this command instead:

COPY C:\WORD*.LTR C:\LETTERS

☛ **Copying Files from a Directory to a Diskette.**
Suppose you needed to print one of your spreadsheets on a printer that is attached to another PC. To do this, you want to copy your spreadsheet file, YEAREND.WK1, from the \SPREADSHT directory to a diskette, then copy the file from that diskette to the other PC. Here are the two commands to accomplish the first part of this task:

CD\SPREADSHT

COPY YEAREND.WK1 A:

To accomplish this in one step, use this command instead:

COPY C:\SPREADSHT\YEAREND.WK1 A:

☛ **Copying Files from a Diskette to a Directory.**
Continuing our scenario, suppose you wanted to copy your spreadsheet file from your diskette to a directory called \123 on the PC with the printer. Enter these commands to change to the diskette drive that holds the file, and copy the file:

A:

COPY YEAREND.WK1 C:\123

To accomplish this in one step, use this command instead:

COPY A:\YEAREND.WK1 C:\123

☛ **Copying Files from One Diskette to Another.**
If your PC has two diskette drives, you can copy files from one diskette to another. Suppose you

have a file called SALES.DOC on a diskette in drive A, and you want to copy that file to a diskette in drive B so you can use that file on a different PC. Start by changing to drive A, and then copy the file to drive B:

A:

COPY SALES.DOC B:

To accomplish this in one step, use this command instead:

COPY A:SALES.DOC B:

Pack Up the U-Haul, We're Moving Files

Moving files from one directory to another is simple with DOS 6.2. In an earlier example, you copied files from the \WORD directory to the \LETTERS directory. With the COPY command, the files resided in two places on your hard disk. To move them instead, you use the MOVE command. The syntax for the MOVE command is similar to the COPY command. You type MOVE, then the file to move, and then the directory you want to move the file to.

Copy Cat!   Like COPY, you don't have to specify where to move the files, but if you don't, DOS will move them to the current directory or drive.

To move those letters from the \WORD directory to the \LETTERS directory, type these commands:

CD\WORD

MOVE *.LTR C:\LETTERS

Don't Move Too Fast!   DOS 6.2 will prompt you if you attempt to move a file on top of an existing copy of the same file. For example, if you move the file HOLYCOW.DOC from your \MOO directory into your \WORD directory and a HOLYCOW.DOC file already exists there, you'll be prompted. Press **Y** to overlay the file, or **N** to abort the move process.

You can include the file path with the MOVE command to perform the move in one step:

MOVE C:\WORD*.LTR C:\LETTERS

And guess what? I don't like moving files this way, either. I just don't like to type that much, I guess. I usually change to the directory where the file is, then use the MOVE command. But you can do it however you want.

Ah, copying and moving files. What fun that was. In the next lesson, you'll learn how to get rid of those unsightly files by deleting them. You'll also learn how to get them back when you didn't mean to delete them.

Lesson 8

Deleting Files (and Getting Them Back)

To Delete or Not to Delete

You will find yourself deleting files for many reasons: the files are outdated and you no longer use them, or you need to make room on your hard drive. Make absolutely sure that you don't need the file any more before you delete it. If your boss asks for a report that you deleted two weeks ago, you'll be in big trouble.

> **This Darn Hard Drive Is All Congested** If you have too many files on your hard drive, copy some of the files onto floppy diskettes and delete them from your hard drive. That way, you still have them around if you need them later. (See Lesson 15 for more on backing up files.)

To delete files, you use the DEL command. The syntax for the DEL command is simple: **DEL** *filename*. (You replace the word *filename* with the name of your file.) For example, say you want to delete the file BALONEY.DOC in the JUNK directory. You would first change to the JUNK directory by typing **CD\JUNK**, and then you would type **DEL BALONEY.DOC**. Presto! The file is deleted.

Don't forget that you can use wild cards here, too. If you type **DEL *.***, you will be deleting all the files in the current directory. Because DOS is so safety-conscious, it will ask you if you are really sure that you want to delete all the files before it starts getting rid of them. Press **Y** for Yes if you are asked for confirmation.

I'm a Worry Wart   If you always want DOS to ask you for confirmation before deleting a file, use the **/P** switch after you type the file name.

You Can't Do That!   If you get a message that says **Access Denied**, that means you can't delete the file. Someone has protected it by making it *read-only*. You can turn off the read-only status of the file by using the ATTRIB command, but the person who protected it probably did it for a good reason, so you better not mess around with it.

Uh-Oh, I Accidentally Deleted the Wrong File

First of all, don't panic if you delete a file by mistake. However, *don't do anything* until you try to get it back. If you've done something crazy, like save or copy documents since you deleted the file, you might not be able to undelete it.

See, DOS doesn't really delete files when you tell it to. It erases the file's *record*: the file's name and location. But unless new data has overwritten the deleted file, it's still there. Still confused? This is how it actually works: when DOS erases the file's name from its records, it merely changes the first letter of its name to a question mark, as in ?ONSENSE.DOC. DOS knows not to pay attention to any file that begins with a question mark, so the space that the file occupies becomes available. If another file needs the disk space, it is written over the deleted file, replacing the old data.

To get back a file that you know the name of, type **UNDELETE** *filename*. Otherwise, type **UNDELETE** ***.*** to list all the recently deleted files. A listing of files will appear, as shown in Figure 8.1. Press **Y** to confirm the undelete procedure. If you don't want to undelete a particular file, press **N**. You might have a whole slew of files if you've just done a lot of deleting. To stop the list, press **Esc**.

I typed the command here.

```
C:\>undelete *.*

UNDELETE - A delete protection facility
Copyright (C) 1987-1993 Central Point Software, Inc.
All rights reserved.

Directory: C:\
File Specifications: *.*

    Delete Sentry control file not found.

    Deletion-tracking file contains   15 deleted files.
    Of those,   13 files have all clusters available,
                 1 files have some clusters available,
                 1 files have no clusters available.

    MS-DOS directory contains   15 deleted files.
    Of those,   14 files may be recovered.

Using the Deletion-tracking method.

    ┌─$MONOTMP PCX      9046 10-08-93 10:14a  ...A  Deleted: 10-08-93 10:19a
All │of the clusters for this file are available. Undelete (Y/N)?
```

The list starts here.

Figure 8.1 *UNDELETE lists recently deleted files.*

If you're asked, politely enter the first letter of the deleted file. DOS will display a message telling you whether you were successful or not.

Lesson 9

Controlling Delinquent Directories When They Get Out of Hand

It's Alive!

All along, I've been talking about directories. And I always told you that soon I would show you how to make your own directories. Well, the time has come. You're ready to create your own little monsters.

It's disgustingly easy to make directories. Use the MD (**m**ake **d**irectory) command. Here's the syntax for the MD command:

MD [*d:*]*path*

The directory you create is placed under the current directory. For example, if you are in the root directory, the directory you create is placed under the root. If you are in a directory called \WORD, the directory you create is placed under the \WORD directory. You catch my drift.

You can create directories in one step, if you want, by adding a path to the MD command, like this:

MD C:\MYSTUFF

Now, suppose you wanted to place the MYSTUFF directory under your WORD directory instead of under the root. All you have to do is change to the WORD directory first, then use the **MD MYSTUFF** command. Or you can use this single command that includes the complete path:

MD C:\WORD\MYSTUFF

Last Name, Please You can add up to a three-letter extension to a directory (as in WORK.93), but this may lead to confusion with file names, which almost always have an extension. Hardly anyone uses extensions in directories. Probably only real weirdos.

Makin' a List, Checkin' It Twice

In Lesson 6, you learned how to list the files in a directory with the DIR command. Directories are also listed when you use the DIR command, and they are denoted with a special **<DIR>** marker.

To list the subdirectories of your current directory, and *not the files*, type **DIR ***. For example, if you change to the root directory and use this command, you'll see the main directories on your hard disk. (Those directories that are just under the root directory.) This enables you to easily familiarize yourself with a new PC.

If you want to see a listing of *all the directories* on a disk, use the TREE command:

TREE [*d*:][*path*][/F][/A] |MORE

For example, to list all the directories on your C drive, type this command:

TREE C:\ |MORE

The Path to Success The TREE command is an external command, and as such, you'll need a path to your \DOS directory in order to use it. See Lesson 4 for more information about paths.

The |MORE parameter at the end of the TREE command is not required, but often necessary because it keeps the listing from scrolling off your screen before you can read it. If you've ever had a list whip by you at warp speed, you know how frustrating it can be. Don't let it happen to you.

This Directory's Gotta Go

In Lesson 8, you learned how to delete just the files in a directory with the DEL command. That's useful if you need to "clean out" a directory without actually removing it. However, sometimes you might want to get rid of the whole blasted thing. In that case you would use the DELTREE command:

DELTREE [/Y][*d:*]*path*

For example, to delete a directory called DUMMY under your WORD directory, use this command:

DELTREE C:\WORD\DUMMY

DOS will prompt you to verify that you really want to delete the directory and all of its files. You do, or else you wouldn't have typed the darn command, so press **Y** to continue. (If you change your mind, press **N** to abort the deletion.)

So Long, Farewell, auf Wiedersehen, Goodnight   If you delete the directory in which files were stored, you may not be able to undelete the files. Be careful.

If you don't care to be prompted, use the /Y switch (which is placed in front of the name of the directory you want to delete), like this: **DELTREE /Y C:\WORD\BIGCO**.

This Directory Needs a New Name

There may be times when you'll want to change the name of a directory. Maybe you didn't get the name right and you keep forgetting what the directory is for, or maybe the purpose of the directory has changed. Maybe you named it something stupid like HOOEY and you can't remember what sort of junk you've got in there. Use the MOVE command:

MOVE [*d:*]*olddir* [*d:*]*newdir*

It sounds weird, I know, but DOS doesn't understand that REN command when you're using directories. That's only for files. You have to move the directory into a new directory. For example, to rename a directory called \1992 to \1993, use this command:

MOVE C:\1992 C:\1993

Oh No! Now What?   If you see the error message **Bad command or file name**, you need to set up a DOS path so that you can use the MOVE command. See Lesson 4 for more details.

You've now learned everything you ever wanted to know about directories. Next you'll learn something very exciting: how to format diskettes. Okay, okay, you can stop jumping up and down, it's not that exciting.

Lesson 10

Somebody's Gotta Do It: Formatting Disks

Do I *Have* to Format My Disks?

You don't have to format your disks. You can shell out the extra clams and buy them preformatted in the store, but you really shouldn't. Not only are you wasting your money paying someone else to do a simple task that you can do yourself in very little time, but disks that are formatted in the drive you'll be using them in are generally more reliable.

When you format diskettes, all you're doing is preparing them for use and erasing all information that might be on them. However, you have to follow more DOS rules (ugh!) when formatting.

First of all, diskettes must be formatted to the proper *density*. In Lesson 2, you learned that the density of a diskette determines the amount of information it can hold. If you use diskettes that match the density of your computer's diskette drives, you won't have to worry about formatting them incorrectly. By default, diskettes are formatted to the density of the drive they occupy.

To format a disk, first place the diskette in the disk drive. Then, use the FORMAT command.

After you type **FORMAT**, type the drive letter to format, followed by a colon (for example, **A:**). Press **Enter**, and you will be prompted to insert the diskette. You've already done that, so press **Enter** again, and DOS attempts to save unformatting information, and then formats the diskette.

After the disk is formatted, you can type an optional volume label, up to 11 characters (including spaces). Press **Enter** when you are through.

To format another diskette of the same density, type **Y** at the **Format another (Y/N)?** prompt, and press **Enter**. After a diskette is formatted, DOS displays the amount of space available on the diskette, as shown in Figure 10.1.

```
C:\>FORMAT B:
Insert new diskette for drive B:
and press ENTER when ready...

Checking existing disk format.
Formatting 1.44M
Format complete.

Volume label (11 characters, ENTER for none)?

    1,457,664 bytes total disk space
    1,457,664 bytes available on disk

        512 bytes in each allocation unit.
      2,847 allocation units available on disk.

Volume Serial Number is 324F-11E1

Format another (Y/N)?
```

Figure 10.1   *DOS displays the amount of space on the formatted diskette.*

Make It Quick   If the diskette has already been formatted, and you simply want to erase the files, use the **/Q** switch after you type the disk drive.

Bootable? What's Bootable?

You can make a *bootable diskette* to boot your system in the case of an emergency. It's a good idea to have one on hand, so you should make one now while you're thinking about it. All you have to add is the /S switch, like this: **FORMAT A: /S**. Then just complete the rest of the formatting steps like usual.

Why Do I Use the /S Switch?   The /S switch tells DOS to copy the *system* files onto the diskette, making it bootable.

Another variation outside the norm of formatting is when you have to format a double-density diskette in a high-density drive. In this situation, you would complete the usual steps for formatting a diskette until you get to the part where you enter the drive letter. After you type in the drive letter, use the /F: switch followed by the size of the diskette in bytes, like this: **FORMAT A: /F:360**. Then you complete the rest of the formatting steps like normal.

Whoopsy-Daisy, I Don't Think I Should Have Formatted That Disk

You might be able to unformat a diskette that you or some lunkhead formatted accidentally. (The creators of DOS just *knew* this was going to happen.) To unformat a diskette, first place the diskette in its drive, and then type **UNFORMAT** *drive:* (where *drive:* is replaced by the letter of the diskette drive). When prompted, type **Y** to proceed with the unformat.

Cross your fingers and hope that it works. If you've done anything to the disk since your formatted it, you might not be able to retrieve the Unformat information. DOS is funny that way.

Whew! I'm glad that whole formatting and unformatting thing is over, how about you? Now you get to learn about all sorts of other handy things you can do with your diskettes.

Lesson 11

Other Handy Things You Can Do with Your Disks

Copying the Whole Blasted Thing

When it comes to disks, less is not necessarily more. The stuff on your disks is probably pretty important, or else you wouldn't have saved it on disk. If you've got a disk that has very important data on it, you should make sure you have more than one copy of the disk. Why? Because if you suddenly get an error message like **General failure reading drive A** (which, by the way, is a very bad thing) when you're trying to look at the very important data, you will not have to pull your hair out and throw a fit. You will have a backup copy of the disk.

You should always make a copy of new program diskettes to keep as a backup in case the originals get damaged in some way. You should also make a copy of your original DOS diskettes. In addition, you may want to copy your own work diskettes as backups.

> **Copy Cat!** When copying diskettes, you must use the same size and density as the original diskette. If you don't, your computer will get confused.

You copy diskettes with the DISKCOPY command:

DISKCOPY *sourcedrive*: *destinationdrive*:

For example, to copy a diskette using drive A, insert the *original diskette* into the drive and type:

DISKCOPY A: A:

The first drive letter is the *source drive* (where the original disk is placed), and the second drive letter is the *target* or *destination drive* (where the target disk is placed). These are often the same drive letters, as in **A: A:**. Be sure to follow both drive letters with a colon, and separate them with a space.

After typing the DISKCOPY command, verify that the source (original) disk is in the drive, and then press **Enter**. When prompted, remove the original diskette, and insert the destination (target) disk in the drive. (You will not have to switch diskettes if you use two different drives.) After the copying procedure is done, you can copy an additional diskette by typing **Y** at the prompt that asks, **Copy another diskette?**

Let's Go for a Drive   You must enter two drive letters (such as A: A:) with the DISKCOPY command, or you will get the error message **Invalid drive specification. Specified drive does not exist or is non-removable.** Sounds scary, but it just means that you forgot to specify the drives. In addition, you can't use a drive letter which indicates a hard disk, such as drive C. You can only use diskette drive letters, such as A: and B:. DOS is funny that way.

You can verify the copy process as it proceeds by adding the **/V** (verify) switch, as in:

DISKCOPY A: A: /V

This slows down the copying process considerably, but it is much safer. You can also compare two diskettes after using the DISKCOPY command, to verify that an exact copy has been made. Simply type

DISKCOMP A: A:, and press **Enter**. (Be sure to use the same drive letters as you did with the DISKCOPY command.) Insert any diskette, wait until prompted, then switch to the other diskette. If there is any difference between the two diskettes, you'll see a message indicating the sector(s) where the difference(s) were found.

Fast Switch   With earlier versions on DOS, you had to switch diskettes several times during the copying process. DOS 6.2 copies information to the hard disk during the copy process so you will only swap diskettes once. How convenient.

Bad Sectors and Other Things That Go Bump in the Night

Eventually, you'll probably get a disk that has bad sectors. This is not usually a big problem, because you can fix them with ScanDisk. Although you can use the ScanDisk command on your diskettes, it is much more important that you use ScanDisk every once in a while on your hard disk, to clean up after DOS.

Checking It Out!   If you have DOS 6.0, the SCANDISK command is not available. Use the CHKDSK command instead: **CHKDSK C: /F**. It does not detect and repair all the problems that ScanDisk does, however, it can repair lost cluster/lost chain problems.

Now, you're probably wondering what clusters and chains are and how they got lost. Well, as you learned in Lesson 8, when you delete a file it's not really deleted. Instead, the reference to where that file is located is erased, and the area is marked "available." Sometimes, DOS is a bit of a slob, and an area will be marked "used" even after the file reference is erased. This creates a *lost cluster* or a *lost chain*.

To clean up these lost chains and clusters, and to make that space available again, use ScanDisk. It can perform a surface scan (to check for physical damage) and check and repair damage to DoubleSpace drives (see Lesson 13). To use ScanDisk to check the status of drive C, for example, *exit all programs first*. This is very important. Then use this command: **SCANDISK C:**

Network News   Don't ever try to use SCANDISK on a network drive, such as drive F. Very horrible things will occur.

You can have ScanDisk verify several drives at once, by simply specifying the drive letters (**SCANDISK C: D:**), or you can use the /**ALL** switch. If you want ScanDisk to check for problems but not to fix them, use the /**CHECKONLY** switch. To check for problems and repair them automatically, use the /**AUTOFIX** switch. So many choices.

As long as you haven't used the /**CHECKONLY** or /**AUTOFIX** switches, ScanDisk will prompt you when it encounters problems, and give you a choice as to how to proceed: Fix It, Don't Fix It, or obtain More Info. To make a choice, press the bold letter, or click on the button with your mouse. For example, to select Fix It, click on it or press **F**.

If your drive has lost clusters or chains, ScanDisk will ask you if you want it to create a file to contain the data that was in each lost cluster, as shown in Figure 11.1. The data is probably unusable because it's part of an old file. You can delete the file by pressing **L** or clicking on Delete. If you'd rather have ScanDisk automatically delete them as they occur, add the **/NOSAVE** switch.

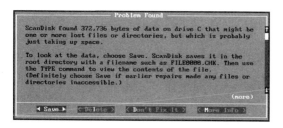

Figure 11.1 *ScanDisk prompts you when it runs across problems.*

At a particular point, ScanDisk will prompt you to insert a *blank* diskette, which you can later use to undo the repairs if you so choose. To later undo the repairs performed by ScanDisk, insert the Undo diskette, and type this command: **SCANDISK C: /UNDO.**

At a later point, ScanDisk will ask you if you want it to perform a surface scan on the disk. This type of scan detects physical errors on the disk, and it should be performed periodically. To perform the scan, press **Enter**. To bypass it, press **N** for No. In addition, you can have ScanDisk perform a surface scan without prompting you by adding the **/SURFACE** switch.

At the end of its program, ScanDisk will allow you to view a log of its results (shown here in Figure 11.2) and to save that log if you want. Simply click View Log (or press **V**), and then **S**ave Log (or press **S**). The log is saved in the file SCANDISK.LOG, and it's located in the root directory of the scanned drive. If you want a detailed explanation of the problems encountered, click on **More** Info, or press **Enter**. To exit ScanDisk, press **x**, or click on Exit. Got all that?

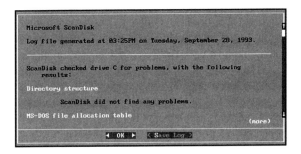

Figure 11.2   You can view a log of ScanDisk's results if you so desire.

I don't know about you, but I've had it up to here with all this ScanDisk stuff. Why they make it so complicated, I have no idea. Let's move on to the next lesson, where you'll learn how to increase the storage space on your hard disk with DBLSPACE.

Lesson 12

Double Your Fun with DoubleSpace

What's a Compressed Drive?

Disk compression programs such as DoubleSpace can store more information on a disk because data is stored more densely than with MS-DOS alone. If you use DoubleSpace, your hard disk can increase its capacity by almost two times. Imagine!

When you install DOS 6.2, your drives are still uncompressed. You must run DoubleSpace to compress a drive. After you install DoubleSpace, your hard disk will consist of two sections, as shown in Figure 12.1. One section will remain uncompressed, to support the few programs and system files that cannot run on a compressed drive.

You can use a drive compressed with DoubleSpace the same way you would use any regular drive; the only difference is that it will store more files than it normally would. Unbelievable? Too good to be true? The next section explains how it's done.

Check Those Utilities   If you depend on third-party utilities such as PC Tools and Norton Utilities, make sure that they are compatible with a DoubleSpace drive. If you're not sure, consult the manual or call the manufacturer before you run these programs.

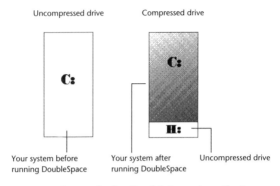

Figure 12.1   Before and after DoubleSpace installation.

How DoubleSpace Works

If you don't care about how DoubleSpace works, you can skip this part. But I'm going to explain it for the skeptics and the people who are just plain curious. After DoubleSpace installation, your drive C is unaltered. But there is a huge file that takes up most of it now. This huge file, called *DBLSPACE.000*, is your compressed drive. DOS assigns a drive letter to this file, so you can access your files from it.

Most Illogical   The DBLSPACE.000 file is not really a drive. DOS pretends that it is, so the files within it can be read normally. A drive that is not physically a drive is called a *logical drive*. Figure that one out.

All the files that were formerly on your hard disk are compressed into DBLSPACE.000, along with most of the free space remaining on the drive. A little bit of free space is left outside of DBLSPACE.000 (uncompressed), in case you need it.

Here's the tricky part. DOS knows that you expect all the files that were on C: before to be accessible from C: now. So, it assigns the drive letter C: to the *compressed* drive, and changes the name of the *real* C: drive to something else (usually H: or I:). That way, you can still do everything from the C: prompt like you did before you compressed your hard disk. Truly incredible!

For Your Protection   The new DOS 6.2 Double-Space includes DoubleGuard, which protects the DoubleSpace data in memory against accidental corruption from errant programs.

I'm Convinced, Now How Do I Use DoubleSpace?

Put up your feet and keep a good book at your side, because this may take a while. It takes roughly one minute per megabyte of data to compress your hard disk, so you might want to start the DoubleSpace setup program at the end of the day and run it overnight.

Scanning for Signs of Life   DOS 6.2 uses ScanDisk (see Lesson 11) to verify the integrity of a drive before it compresses it. (This reduces the risk of problems later on.) DOS 6.0 users had to run a disk utility, such as Norton Utilities or PC Tools, to verify disk's integrity before running DoubleSpace. ScanDisk is just another of the many ways Microsoft is trying to make us happy.

To set up DoubleSpace, first you have to exit all programs. Then, change to the DOS directory by typing **CD\DOS** and pressing **Enter**. Start the DoubleSpace setup program by typing **DBLSPACE** and pressing **Enter**.

Choose between *Custom* or *Express* setup. (Unless you are an experienced user, select *Express* setup.) A small section of your drive will remain uncompressed. If you want to change the default letter for the uncompressed drive, do so before pressing **Enter**.

A message will appear which tells you how long the compression process will take. Press **C** to Continue (which will complete the compression process) or **Esc** to exit (which will stop it).

After the disk compression is finished, a summary will be displayed, showing information on the compressed drive. Press **Enter** and your system will restart with the compressed drive active. There you go!

Now that you have a compressed drive, you use it as normal. Copy programs or files, create or delete directories, or delete files as normal.

Is There No Looking Back? With the old DoubleSpace (DOS 6.0), the process could not be reversed unless you reformatted your hard drive. That's not always a pleasant option, so Microsoft came up with a better way to reverse the compression process. You can decompress a drive (assuming you have enough room) by using the **Tools Uncompress** command within the DoubleSpace utility. (See Lesson 13 for details on using the DoubleSpace utility.)

Okay, now that your drive is compressed, let's look at a bunch of cool things you can do with it. You'll learn how to run the DoubleSpace utility program and how to compress a floppy diskette in the next lesson.

Lesson 13

But Wait, There's More You Can Do with DoubleSpace

Now That I Have a Compressed Drive, What Do I Do with It?

In Lesson 12, you learned how to compress your disk drive. But now that it's compressed, what do you do? Well, you work with your compressed drive as you would with any other drive. The compression process remains invisible to you, the user. It's actually quite fascinating. Instead of rambling on about how great it is, however, I'll just get down to the nitty-gritty.

The DoubleSpace utility program lets you perform these compression functions:

- ☛ Increase the storage capacity of diskettes by compressing them.
- ☛ Adjust the size of your compressed drive.
- ☛ Display information about the compressed drive.
- ☛ Format a compressed drive.
- ☛ Defragment a compressed drive. (You'll learn more about defragmenting a drive in Lesson 14.)
- ☛ Check a compressed drive's integrity.

Let's get started. First, access the DoubleSpace utility program by typing **DBLSPACE** at the DOS prompt. A new kind of screen will pop up. To open a menu and issue a command, simply click on the menu to open it, and click on a command. With the keyboard, press **Alt** and hold it down, and then press the bold letter in the menu you want to open. For example, to open the Tools menu, press **Alt+T**. Once a menu is open, press the underlined letter of the command to select it.

To exit the DoubleSpace utility program, open the Drive menu by clicking on it or pressing **Alt+D**. Then select the Exit command by clicking on it or pressing X.

Compressing a Diskette

You can use DoubleSpace to increase the storage capacity of your *high-density* diskettes (you can't use DoubleSpace on a double-density diskette). This is a pretty cool way to cram even more stuff on your disks.

Compression Depression　You can only use a compressed diskette on a PC that uses DOS 6 or 6.2, and is running DoubleSpace. That means that if you copy files onto a disk for someone else to use, make sure that person has a compressed drive as well.

Don't Touch That Dial!　If you use DOS 6.0, do not remove the double-spaced diskette or reboot your PC while you are using a compressed diskette. If you do, you will need to use the Mount command to make the diskette available again. Simply insert the diskette, start the DoubleSpace utility, open the Drive menu, and select the Mount command. If you use DOS 6.2, you don't need to worry about mounting or unmounting—compressed diskettes are recognized automatically by the system.

You can only compress a diskette if you have already run the DoubleSpace setup program (see Lesson 12). To compress a diskette, first insert the diskette in its drive. Then, type **DBLSPACE** at the DOS prompt, and press **Enter**.

Open the **Compress** menu, and select the **Existing Drive** command. The dialog box shown in Figure 13.1 is displayed.

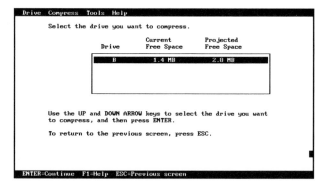

Figure 13.1 Compressing a diskette is terribly easy.

You can return to DOS by selecting the **Exit** command from the **Drive** menu. When the disk has been compressed, you can use it as you would any other.

Yikes! I Didn't Mean to Compress My Drive!

Whoops! You compressed your drive and then changed your mind. Fortunately, DOS 6.2 comes with an "uncompress" feature (the 6.0 version didn't have it). If you want to go back to your old, uncompressed drive, first make sure you have enough room on your disk to store the uncompressed files. Also, you should back up the compressed drive's files. (See Lesson 15 for more information.)

To uncompress a drive, type **DBLSPACE** and press **Enter**. Then, open the Tools menu, and select the Uncompress command. Follow the additional instructions on the screen. When it's done, Shazam! Your drive will no longer be compressed.

Information, Please

You can display information about your compressed drive, such as the amount of available space, the amount of defragmentation (see Lesson 14 for more information), and the compression ratio (the ratio of compressed disk space to formerly uncompressed space—a compression ratio of 2:1 would reflect a drive whose space had exactly *doubled* through disk compression.)

To look at your disk's compression information, first type **DBLSPACE** at the DOS prompt, and press **Enter**. Open the Drive menu, and select the Info command. The dialog box shown in Figure 13.2 is displayed.

You can list the compression ratio for individual files with a variation of the DIR command: **DIR** /C. When you add the /C switch, you see the compression ratio for each file, as shown in Figure 13.3.

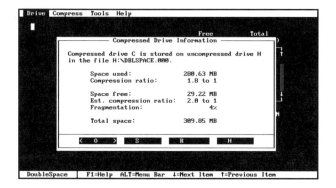

Figure 13.2 *Here's my disk's compression information.*

Compression ratio for this file

```
C:\PM5>dir *.pm5 /c

 Volume in drive C has no label
 Volume Serial Number is 0FD5-0C5F
 Directory of C:\PM5

SAMPLE   PM5     323,456 07-14-93  11:40a   2.1 to 1.0
TOC      PM5      35,968 07-12-93   9:51a   4.7 to 1.0
FIGLOG   PM5      69,248 10-07-93   3:04p   4.5 to 1.0
JACK     PM5       9,152 07-19-93   9:06a   5.3 to 1.0
            2.5 to 1.0 average compression ratio
         4 file(s)       437,824 bytes
                      30,621,696 bytes free

C:\PM5>
```

Total compression ratio for the files listed.

Figure 13.3 *You can display file compression information with the DIR command. How handy.*

I'm finally finished talking about DoubleSpace. Now you get to learn how to check your disks for defragmentation problems with DEFRAG.

Lesson 14

Defragment That Messy Drive

What Does "Defragment" Mean?

Well, it's not as complicated as it sounds. When a file is copied onto a drive by DOS, parts of the file are often split over different sections of the drive in order to make the most effective use of available space. When lots of little parts are spread all over your disk, it is said to be *fragmented*. Thus, *defragmenting* a drive causes those parts of files that were split up to be put back together.

On an uncompressed drive, fragmentation can cause a drop in speed when accessing files. This is because when a file is fragmented (split up) over a drive, it takes longer to locate and read each separate part of the file. If the file is placed on the drive in consecutive sections, the entire file can be read much more quickly. See how it works?

Actually, defragmenting a compressed drive may not affect speed as much as on an uncompressed drive, but it will usually result in additional available space on the drive. This is because a compressed drive is really just one big file, and reorganizing it doesn't really reduce the amount of speed necessary to locate that single file on the drive. But, because of the space thing, it's usually a good idea to defragment a compressed drive periodically.

Okay Then, How Do I Do It?

To defragment an uncompressed drive, first you have to exit all programs (including Windows). Then, use the DEFRAG command, like this: **DEFRAG *d*: [/U] [/S*sortorder*]**.

For example, to defragment drive C, type this command: **DEFRAG C:**. DEFRAG will analyze the drive and make a recommendation for the best optimization method. Press **Enter** to begin optimization. You'll see a message telling you when the drive is optimized. Press **Enter** to continue. You can then optimize another drive, re-optimize this drive using a different optimization method, or exit the DEFRAG utility. It's all up to you. Use the arrow keys to choose an option, and press **Enter** to select it.

Tick, Tick, Tick   The defragmenting process is actually very fast, but if you are defragmenting a huge hard drive, it will take quite a bit of time. The last time I fully defragmented my hard drive, it took almost an hour. (If you just do the minimal defragment, it doesn't take nearly that long.) Make sure you have enough time available if you want to do an optimum defragment.

Organization Specialization

By default, DEFRAG reorganizes the files on the drive so that any empty space is located at one end of the drive. This arrangement takes a bit more time to accomplish, as I'm sure you could guess. If you want to have DEFRAG relocate all the pieces of a file so that they are together, but you don't care if some empty spaces exist between files, use the /U option, like this: **DEFRAG C: /U**.

You can specify the order in which files are organized on the drive. Normally, files are organized in the order in which they are located. To specify a sort order for the files, use the /S switch. The sort order does not affect the physical order of the files on the drive, but it changes the way they are displayed when you type DIR to list files.

There are many options for the /S switch:

- ☞ N or –N   Sorts files by file name.
- ☞ E or –E   Sorts files by extension.
- ☞ D or –D   Sorts files by date and time of last change.
- ☞ S or –S   Sorts files by size.

Placing a minus sign in front of an option causes a reverse order to be used. For example, **DEFRAG C: /SN** sorts files alphabetically by size and file name, while **DEFRAG C: /S–N** sorts files in reverse alphabetical order by file name.

A Special Tip for DoubleSpace Users

You can't just go around defragmenting the regular way if you have a compressed drive. You have to use the DoubleSpace utility to defragment your drive. Remember, defragmenting a compressed drive will not necessarily result in an increase in speed, but it might possibly increase the available space on the compressed drive.

First of all, type **DBLSPACE** at the DOS prompt, and press **Enter**. Then, open the Tools menu, and select the Defragment command. You'll see a message asking whether you really want to do this. Click on **Yes**, or press **Enter** to continue. After the drive is defragmented, open the Drive menu, and select Exit to return to DOS. It's that easy.

Well, your drives are now all optimized and defragmented. Next, you'll learn how to back up your important files.

Lesson 15

Backup: A Computer Plumbing Problem or a Precaution?

An Overview of Backup

Here's another great feature that comes with DOS 6.2: MS Backup. It's much easier to use than the BACKUP command from versions prior to DOS 6. Even if you've performed backups with an earlier DOS version, you should read both this and the next lesson in order to familiarize yourself with the MS Backup utility. If you upgraded from DOS 6.0, there is some good news: MS Backup is exactly the same as it was in that version, and you can skip these next two lessons. Get a candy bar or something and take a break.

A *backup* is a copy of the files on your hard disk. There are three types of backups:

- **Full backup**   This backup is a complete copy of every file on your hard disk.

- **Incremental backup**   This backup copies only the files that have been changed since the last full or incremental backup. To restore a complete hard disk, you would need *your full backup and all incremental backup diskettes.*

- **Differential backup**   This backup copies only the files that have been changed since the last full backup. A differential backup may take longer than an incremental backup. To restore a complete hard disk, *you would need your full backup and latest differential backup diskettes.*

Here's a Plan   As a good rule, perform a full backup once a month, then perform either an incremental or differential backup at the end of each work day. If you don't perform your full backups often, use an incremental backup every day because it won't take as long as a differential backup.

When a backup is performed, a *backup catalog* is created. It's a little bit like the Spiegel catalog, but you can't order slacks from it. You can only look at information about what was backed up and when. The backup catalog is copied to both the hard disk and the last backup diskette. The backup catalog is used when restoring files.

To perform a backup, you must select the drives, directories, and the files to be backed up. These selections can be stored permanently in a *setup file*, so you can reuse them at a later date. MS Backup comes with a few setup files already created for common situations, such as a full backup. Apparently, "Convenience" is DOS's new middle name.

The first time you run MS Backup, it will configure itself. To do this, MS Backup will run some tests on your system. You will need two diskettes of the same size and density as the diskettes you will use when you do real backups. Follow the on-screen instructions, and remember to save the configuration when the tests are over. And yes, you *have* to do the tests.

I Want It All: Performing a Full Backup

In case you have never dealt with a Windows-like environment, here's how you'll make selections within the MS Backup utility:

- *With a mouse,* simply click on an option to select it.

- *With the keyboard,* press and hold the **Alt** key. Then press the **bold letter** of the option you want to select.

Now let's begin. First, type **MSBACKUP** at the DOS prompt, and press **Enter**. Choose **Backup**, and pow! The Backup dialog box, shown in Figure 15.1, appears.

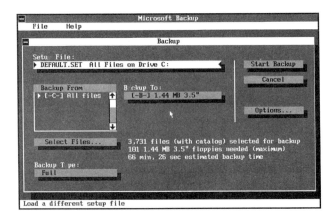

Figure 15.1 *You can configure your backup from the Backup dialog box.*

In the **Backup From** box, select the drive to back up. MS Backup will display **All Files** next to the drive letter you select. Choose any additional drives if you want. If you are going to use diskettes of a type or size different from the one listed, change the drive letter in the **Backup To** box.

When you're ready to roll, select **Start Backup**. When the backup is complete, press **Enter** and select Quit to return to DOS.

Incremental and Differential Equations

Why does the word "differential" always seem to go with the word "equations" in my mind? It must be left-over trauma from high school calculus class. (Or was that trigonometry? I can never remember.) Either way, a differential backup is absolutely nothing like a differential equation. Thank heavens.

Differential backs up any file that has been changed since the last full backup; *incremental* backs up only those files that have been changed since either a full or incremental backup (whichever was more recent). Performing an incremental or differential backup of your entire hard disk is easy:

Do this: type **MSBACKUP** at the DOS prompt, and press **Enter**. Then, choose **Backup**, and the Backup dialog appears. In the **Backup From** box, select the drive to back up. MS Backup will display **All Files** next to the drive letter you select.

Select any additional drives if you want. If you are going to use diskettes of a type or size different from the one listed, change the drive letter in the **Backup To** box. In the **Backup Type** box, select **Incremental** or **Differential**.

When you've done everything and you're ready to go, select **Start Backup**. When the backup is complete, press **Enter** and select Quit to return to DOS.

Not Those Files, *These* Files

Say you want to back up only certain directories or files. Since all your program files are on the original diskettes, and they don't change, why back them up? By backing up only the directories which contain the files you create, you can reduce the time it takes to do a full backup.

Safety First You may want one full backup of your system (complete with program files) in case of hard drive failure.

To back up selected directories or files, first go to the Backup dialog box by using the MSBACKUP command and choosing **Backup**. If you are going to use diskettes of a type or size different from the one listed, change the drive letter in the **Backup To** box. In the **Backup Type** box, select **Full**, **Incremental**, or **Differential**.

If necessary, in the **Backup From** box, select the drive whose files you want to back up. Choose **Select Files**, and the Select Backup Files dialog box appears. Select the directories or files to back up:

With the mouse Double-click (or click with the right mouse button) on a file or directory to select it. To select multiple files or directories, click the left mouse button and hold, click the right mouse button, then drag until the group is selected.

With the keyboard Use the Spacebar to select directories or files.

Make Your Selection, Please An arrow indicates selected directories. If all the files in a directory are not selected, it is displayed with a double arrow. A check mark indicates selected files within a directory. That should explain things a little better.

When you are done selecting files, select **OK**. Then, select **Start Backup**. When the backup is complete, press **Enter** and select Quit to return to DOS. See, that wasn't so hard, was it?

You can also select files by using Include and Exclude in the Select Backup Files dialog box. Select Include or Exclude, then enter a directory path, such as **C:\WORD\DOCS**. Next, enter a file name pattern, such as ***.DOC**. Decide whether to include or exclude subdirectories, and then select **OK**.

What good is a backup if you don't know how to use it? Well, in the next lesson, you'll learn how to use your backup to restore files to your hard disk if they get damaged.

Lesson 16

Yikes! My Hard Disk Is Ruined! (How Do I Get It Back?)

Restoring a Full Backup When There's No Other Way

Are you sure you need to restore your hard drive? You didn't accidentally forget to turn the power on? Did you try turning your computer off and on? Well, if nothing else works and you have to restore everything, do this:

First, type **MSBACKUP** at the DOS prompt, and press **Enter**. Choose **Restore**, and the Restore dialog box, as shown in Figure 16.1, appears.

In the **Restore Files** box, select the drive to restore. Use the drive that the files were backed up from, regardless of whether you want to restore the files to a different drive. **All Files** will display next to the drive letter you select.

Select any additional drives if you want. If you are going to use diskettes of a type or size different from the one listed, change the drive letter in the **Restore From** box. If you want to restore files to different drives or directories from which they were backed up, select **Restore To**.

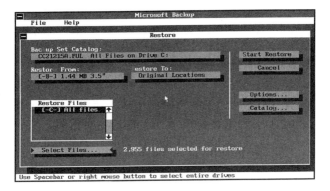

Figure 16.1 *You can configure your restoration from the Restore dialog box. What a deal!*

When you're finished setting everything up, select **Start Restore**. When the restore is complete, press **Enter** and select **Quit** to return to DOS. That was not quite as painful as you originally thought, I'm sure.

I Don't Want to Restore the Whole Thing

By restoring only the files or directories you need, you can reduce the time it takes to do a full restore. As with everything else, you have to type **MSBACKUP** at the DOS prompt, and press **Enter** before you can do anything.

When you choose **Restore** and the Restore dialog box appears, change the options. If you are going to use diskettes of a type or size different from the one listed, change the drive letter in the **Restore From** box. If necessary, in the **Restore Files** box, select the drive whose files you want to restore. Use the drive that the files were backed up from, regardless of whether you want to restore the files to a different drive.

Choose **Select Files**, and the Select Restore Files dialog box appears. From there, select the directories or files to restore:

With the mouse Double-click (or click with the right mouse button) on a file or directory to select it. To select multiple files or directories, click the left mouse button and hold, click the right mouse button, then drag until the group is selected. To select noncontiguous files or directories, press **Ctrl**, and click on each item.

With the keyboard Use the **Spacebar** to select directories or files.

Make Your Selection, Please Selected directories display with an arrow. If all the files in a directory are not selected, the directory is displayed with a double arrow. Selected files within the directory display with a check mark. That should clear things up a bit.

When you are done selecting files, select **OK**. If you want to restore files to different drives or directories from which they were backed up, select **Restore To**. Select **Start Restore**. When the restore is complete, press **Enter** and select **Q**uit to return to DOS.

If more than one version of a file exists on your different backup sets, the most recent version is the one DOS restores. You can select a different version by using **Version** from the Select Restore Files dialog box.

In this lesson, you learned how to restore files if they become damaged. In the next lesson, you will learn how to keep your system safe from viruses.

Lesson 17

Viruses Getting You Down?

Should I See a Doctor About This?

No, silly, it's not *that* kind of virus. A computer *virus* is a program that infects your computer in various ways, such as changing your files, damaging your disks, and preventing your computer from starting. They are horrible things created by people who apparently have too much time on their hands and who were evidently mentally traumatized at one time or another and feel that they have to take it out on unsuspecting innocents. Whatever the reason for their existence, viruses are out there, and you have to watch out for them.

You can infect your system any time you copy or download files onto your disk, or boot from a diskette. You can protect yourself from serious damage by:

- ☞ Maintaining a recent backup of your files.
- ☞ Checking diskettes for viruses before copying files from them. *Be sure to check shareware program disks before installing new software.*
- ☞ Write-protecting program diskettes to prevent infection.
- ☞ Running VSafe, a special DOS 6.2 virus-detection program, all the time.
- ☞ Never starting your computer with a diskette in the drive. (Make a virus-free bootable diskette for emergency purposes—see the next section.)
- ☞ Running Microsoft Anti-Virus (another DOS 6.2 program) as soon as a problem occurs.

Creating a Startup Diskette

You can create a virus-safe startup diskette by following the instructions in Lesson 10. After the diskette is formatted, add the following files:

- ☛ CONFIG.SYS
- ☛ AUTOEXEC.BAT
- ☛ MSAV.EXE
- ☛ MSAV.HLP
- ☛ MSAVHELP.OVL

After you've copied these files onto the diskette, write-protect it to prevent infection. If you ever need the diskette, you'll have a good copy of your system files and the virus detection program. Remember to update your AUTOEXEC.BAT and CONFIG.SYS files if you modify them later.

Scanning for Viruses

If you suspect a virus, immediately exit all programs, including Windows. Then, boot your system with your startup diskette. At the DOS prompt, type **MSAV /A /C** and press **Enter**. (If you are connected to a network, type **MSAV /L /C**. This will limit scanning to local drives only). The Anti-Virus main menu appears, as shown in Figure 17.1. All local drives are scanned and cleaned of any viruses found. After the scan is complete, press **F3** to exit. Whew! Close one.

If any viruses are detected, a dialog box will appear, offering several options:

- ☛ Choose Clean to clean the virus from your system.

☞ Choose Continue to ignore the virus, but continue scanning. If you know that a file was changed legitimately, use this option or Update.

☞ Choose Stop to stop the scanning process and go to the Anti-Virus main menu.

☞ Choose Delete to delete the infected file from your system. Use this option if the file has been destroyed by a virus, and you want to prevent further infection.

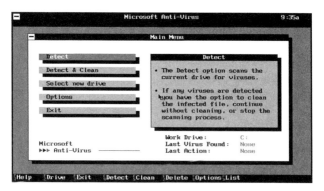

Figure 17.1 *Select scanning options from the Anti-Virus screen.*

Controlling the Virus Scan

If you prefer to control the virus scanning manually, type **MSAV** at the prompt. From the Anti-Virus Main Menu, select from among these options:

☞ If necessary, press **F2** or choose **Select new drive** to change the drive you want to check for viruses.

- ☛ Press **F8** or choose Options to change various scanning options, such as disabling the alarm sound and creating a report of the virus scan.

- ☛ Start the scan by selecting either **Detect** (**F4**) or **Detect & Clean** (**F5**). If you choose Detect, you will be able to select a course of action if an infected file is detected.

Can I Make This Thing Scan Automatically at Startup?

Sure. To perform a scan of your hard disk every time you boot your computer, add the following commands to your AUTOEXEC.BAT file (for more information on editing your AUTOEXEC.BAT file, see Lesson 20):

```
MSAV /N
IF ERRORLEVEL 86 GOTO VIRUSDETECT
ECHO Relax. No viruses were detected.
GOTO END
:VIRUSDETECT
ECHO Viruses were detected. Run MSAV /A /
C.
:END
```

If you are attached to a network, use this command instead:

```
MSAV /N /L
IF ERRORLEVEL 86 GOTO VIRUSDETECT
ECHO Relax. No viruses were detected.
GOTO END
:VIRUSDETECT
ECHO Viruses were detected. Run MSAV /L /C.
:END
```

With one of these commands in place, your hard disk will be scanned automatically at startup, and you'll see a message telling you whether or not you need to run MSAV to clean viruses off your system. See? Easy.

Continuous Detection and Prevention

Using the MSAV command at startup will only detect viruses that are active at that time. To have ongoing protection, run VSafe. VSafe is a program that runs in the background as you perform your normal computer tasks. VSafe will warn you of changes to your files that might be caused by viruses. To start VSafe automatically every time you boot your computer, add this command to your AUTOEXEC.BAT (for more information on editing your AUTOEXEC.BAT file, see Lesson 20): **VSAFE.** That's it.

Did you ever think computing would be so dangerous? Hopefully, you'll never have to worry about viruses again. In the next lesson, you'll learn how to improve your PC's memory usage.

Lesson 18

Making the Most of Memory

Memory? I Forget—What Is It?

Your computer comes with two kinds of memory: *RAM* (random-access memory) and *ROM* (read-only memory). ROM stores the permanent instructions your computer needs to operate. RAM is a temporary storage area used by your programs. It's temporary because everything that's stored in it gets erased when you turn off your computer.

When you start a program, it's loaded into RAM, and it starts executing instructions. As you work on a letter or some other file, that file is kept in RAM so changes can be made. If you create large documents, your program requires large amounts of RAM to manipulate the information in the document. Your program loads other files into RAM as needed. If you spell-check your letter, for example, the spell-check program is loaded into memory where the main program can use it.

All programs need memory in order to run—some need quite a lot of memory. Not having enough memory can affect the way your programs work and even prevent some programs from starting. Kind of like the way humans work. It is vital that you make the most of the memory your computer has.

How Much Memory Does Your Computer Have?

Memory is divided into *bytes*. A byte stores a single character, such as the letter Q. A *kilobyte* (1KB) is roughly 1,000 bytes (it's really 1,024 bytes.) A *megabyte* (1MB) is roughly 1,000,000 bytes (it's really 1,048,576 bytes). RAM is divided into several areas:

- ☞ **Conventional memory** The first 640KB of RAM. Conventional is the most important area of memory because it's the only part of memory in which a program can run.

- ☞ **Upper memory** Memory above 640KB and below 1MB. Usually this area is reserved for your system's use, but pockets of unused space (called *upper memory blocks*) can be converted for use by device drivers and memory-resident (TSRs, or terminate-and-stay-resident) programs.

What's a Device Driver? It's a special program that controls optional devices, such as a mouse or a network card.

- ☞ **Extended memory** Memory above 1MB; it cannot be used to run programs, but only to store data temporarily. Only certain special programs (such as Windows, DESQview, and AutoCAD) can use this area of memory. Programs such as these don't access extended memory through DOS, but through a special extended-memory manager, such as EMM386.EXE (which comes with DOS 5 and above). The capability to access extended memory through an extended-memory manager must be written into an application specifically. Otherwise, that program will not use extended memory, even if you load EMM386.EXE.

☞ **Upper memory** The first 64KB of extended memory. With the help of an upper-memory manager, such as HIMEM.SYS, DOS can access this area of extended memory directly. Upper memory is a good place to store device drivers, memory resident programs, or even DOS itself.

☞ **Expanded memory** Special memory that is linked to DOS through a window in upper memory. As with extended memory, programs can use expanded memory only indirectly through the use of an expanded memory manager, and it is much slower than extended memory.

To see how much memory your system has (and of what type), type **MEM** and press **Enter**. A listing similar to Figure 18.1 will appear. From this listing, you can determine the amount of each kind of memory being used (Adapter RAM/ROM is memory located on add-on boards, such as video boards.)

```
C:\>MEM

Memory Type        Total  =  Used  +  Free
                  -------    ------    ------
Conventional       640K       127K      513K
Upper              187K        81K      106K
Reserved           384K       384K        0K
Extended (XMS)   2,885K     1,241K    1,644K
                  -------    ------    ------
Total memory     4,096K     1,833K    2,263K

Total under 1 MB   827K       208K      619K

Largest executable program size      513K (525,056 bytes)
Largest free upper memory block      105K (107,904 bytes)
MS-DOS is resident in the high memory area.

C:\>
```

Figure 18.1   See how much memory your system has?

To display a listing of programs (shown in Figure 18.2) currently loaded into memory, type this: **MEM /C /P**. The /P switch tells the MEM command to list only one screen's worth of information at a time. To see the next screenful of information, press **Enter**.

```
Modules using memory below 1 MB:

Name        Total     =    Conventional  +   Upper Memory

MSDOS       17,389   (17K)    17,389   (17K)       0    (0K)
SETVER         784    (1K)       784    (1K)       0    (0K)
HIMEM        1,168    (1K)     1,168    (1K)       0    (0K)
EMM386       3,120    (3K)     3,120    (3K)       0    (0K)
COMMAND      2,928    (3K)     2,928    (3K)       0    (0K)
SHARE       14,848   (15K)    14,848   (15K)       0    (0K)
SAVE        72,592   (71K)    72,592   (71K)       0    (0K)
MOUSE       17,088   (17K)    17,088   (17K)       0    (0K)
ANSI         4,208    (4K)         0    (0K)   4,208    (4K)
DBLSPACE    37,712   (37K)         0    (0K)  37,712   (37K)
SMARTDRV    27,408   (27K)         0    (0K)  27,408   (27K)
DOSKEY       4,144    (4K)         0    (0K)   4,144    (4K)
UNDELETE     9,632    (9K)         0    (0K)   9,632    (9K)
Free       633,424  (619K)   525,248  (513K) 108,176  (106K)

Memory Summary:

Type of Memory      Total    =    Used    +   Free

Press any key to continue . . .
```

Figure 18.2   Which programs are using memory?

Maximizing Memory with MemMaker

MemMaker is a diagnostic program that comes with DOS 6 and DOS 6.2. It's designed to optimize the way your system uses memory by changing your configuration files. In order to use MemMaker, you must have a 386 or 486 processor and extended memory.

MemMaker is very easy to use, and it provides fairly good results. To optimize your system with MemMaker, first type **MEMMAKER** at the DOS prompt, and press **Enter**. A screen appears, welcoming you to MemMaker.

When you press **Enter**, a message appears asking you to choose between *Express* (the easiest) and *Custom* (for confident users) optimization. To use Express,

press **Enter**. To switch to Custom, press the **Spacebar**, and then **Enter**. The Express option works well for most systems. It works well for most people, too, especially those of us who don't really know what we're doing.

A message appears, asking you if you use any programs that require expanded memory. Press **Y** for Yes, or **N** for No. Press **Enter** to continue. (If you don't know whether or not you need expanded memory, check your owner's manual.)

When you press **Enter**, MemMaker will reboot your computer and verify your current configuration. It makes changes to your AUTOEXEC.BAT and CONFIG.SYS (your old files are saved with a .UMB extension.) Press **Enter**, and MemMaker will test your new configuration.

MemMaker Blues? If your system locks up (freezes) while MemMaker is testing, you can reboot your system, and MemMaker will pick up where it left off. To reboot, press **Ctrl+Alt+Delete**.

Wait until a message appears, asking whether your new configuration is OK. Press **Y** for Yes or **N** for No. Press **Enter** to continue. If there is a problem, MemMaker can undo its changes or allow you to do further testing. Press **Enter** to undo changes (MemMaker will ask you to confirm), or press the **Spacebar** and then **Enter** to keep the changes. A listing showing your system's memory usage appears. Press **Enter** to exit MemMaker.

Tip

Memories . . . To undo the changes made by MemMaker at any time, type **MEMMAKER /UNDO** and press **Enter**. Ta-dah! Your old configuration is back.

Memory all maximized now? Good, because we have a couple more things to cover before this book is finished. The next lesson deals with DOS's Editor, which is called EDIT.

Lesson 19

DOS's Very Own Editor

Whoa! Slow Down, Turbo

Let me give you a couple of helpful hints before you go around editing everything in sight. When you edit your configuration files, keep these things in mind:

- Do not edit CONFIG.SYS or AUTOEXEC.BAT without a startup diskette handy. Instructions for making a boot-startup diskette are covered in Lesson 10 and Lesson 18.

- It's a good idea to make a backup copy of startup files before you edit them.

- If you make changes to a configuration file, make sure you reboot your PC to make those changes effective.

Okay, Now You Can Edit

An easy-to-use, full-screen text editor called EDIT (the DOS Editor) comes with DOS 6 and DOS 6.2. Although it is beyond the scope of this book to teach you everything you might need to know about using EDIT, this lesson will teach you enough to edit simple files such as CONFIG.SYS and AUTOEXEC.BAT.

First of all, change to the directory which holds the file you want to edit. (To edit CONFIG.SYS or AUTOEXEC.BAT, change to the root directory.) Type **EDIT** and press the **Spacebar**. Then, type the name of the file you want to edit, and press **Enter** to execute the command. The file you requested is opened, as Figure 19.1 shows.

Figure 19.1   The AUTOEXEC.BAT file is ready to edit.

Making Change

Once a file is open, you can make changes to it (obviously, this is where the "edit" part comes in). Although there are many ways to move around the screen, the most commonly used methods are those shown in Table 19.1:

Table 19.1   Moving around the DOS Editor.

To Move:	Press:
Up, down, left, or right	Arrow keys
To the beginning of a line	Home key
To the end of a line	End key
To the beginning of the next line	Ctrl+Enter
To the top of the window	Ctrl+Q, then E
To the bottom of the window	Ctrl+Q, then X

When you start the DOS Editor, you are in *Insert mode*. That means when you position your cursor and start to type, what you type is inserted at that point. If you want to type over existing characters, press the **Insert** key. You are now in *Overtype mode*. Change back to Insert mode by pressing **Insert** again.

If you want to delete some characters, position your cursor on any character, and use the **Delete** key. Zap. It's gone.

To insert a blank line before the line the cursor is on, position your cursor at the beginning of an existing line and press **Enter**.

You Changed It, Now Save It

After making changes to your file, you must save it before exiting the Editor. To save your changes, open the File menu, and select **S**ave.

If you want to keep your original file intact (without changes) and save this file under a new name, choose the Save **A**s from the File menu. Type the new file name, and press **Enter**.

Exiting the DOS Editor

After you have saved your changes, you can safely exit the Editor. Just open the File menu, and select E**x**it. You will be returned to the DOS prompt.

There. In and out of the DOS Editor in no time flat. In the next lesson, you will learn more than you ever wanted to know about configuration. The word alone gives me the willies.

Appendix A

The DOS Shell in a Nutshell

The DOS Shell is a graphical interface that makes it easier to issue common DOS commands such as COPY, MOVE, and DEL. You can even start multiple programs from the Shell and switch between them. DOS 6.2 does not come with the Shell, but if you are upgrading from an earlier version of DOS, you can copy it from your OLD_DOS.1 directory into your new DOS directory. (The OLD_DOS.1 directory was created when you installed DOS 6.2.)

The DOS Shell Environment

You can start the DOS Shell by typing **DOSSHELL**. That shouldn't be too hard to remember.

With a Little Help from Your Friends   You can get additional help at any time while you're in the DOS Shell. Simply press **F1**. Press **Esc** to exit a Help screen.

Off to a Slow Start   If you get the error message **Bad command or file name**, you need to set up a DOS path. See Lesson 4.

The Tree menu is used to expand and contract subdirectories. For example, in Figure XA.2, the TRASH directory is expanded, showing subdirectories. A minus indicates a directory which is displaying its subdirectories, and a plus indicates a directory which is hiding them. Use the plus and the minus keys to expand and contract a directory.

When you start the DOS Shell, it starts in text mode (a display mode that uses lines and such to show screen elements). If your PC has a monitor that supports graphics, you can change the DOS Shell display to graphics mode (a display mode that uses pictures and boxes to show screen elements).

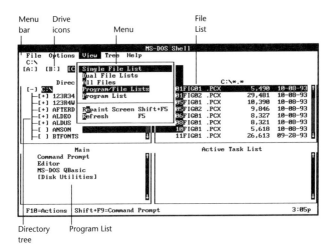

Figure A.1   *The DOS 6 Shell. Oooh. Aaah.*

You can also select from several screen resolutions, which determine the number of text lines that fix on your screen at once. The higher the resolution you select, the smaller (and harder to read!) the text on your screen will appear.

To change the DOS Shell to a different video mode, open the Options menu (press **Alt+O**), and select the Display command (press **D**). Choose the mode you want by either clicking on it or using the arrow keys to highlight it. Click on **OK**, or press **Enter**. The screen changes to the resolution you selected.

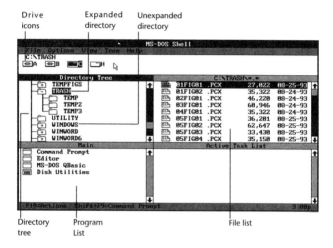

Drive icons   Expanded directory   Unexpanded directory

Directory tree   Program List   File list

Figure A.2 *Here's what the Shell looks like in graphics mode.*

Using the Mouse

The easiest way to use the Shell is with a mouse. To use the mouse, you either *click* or *double-click* with the left mouse button. That means to press the mouse button once (click) or twice quickly (double-click). Some actions require that you *drag* the mouse. That means you first move the mouse to the starting position, and then click and hold the mouse button. Drag the mouse to the ending position, and then release the mouse button. There you go.

Barking Out Commands

One of the best things about the DOS Shell is that you don't type commands; instead, you just select something off a menu, such as the one shown in Figure XA.1. The Shell menu bar contains five choices: File, Options, View, Tree, and Help. To open a menu, just click on the menu name with your mouse.

Once the menu is open, you can select a command by clicking on the command name with your mouse.

Getting There from Here

To work in an area of the Shell, you must move the cursor to that area. Moving the cursor to an area activates the area.

The Shell screen is divided into several areas:

- ☛ **Drive Icons area**   Where you choose which drive to show.
- ☛ **Directory Tree**   Shows the directories on the chosen drive.
- ☛ **File List**   Shows the files in the chosen directory.
- ☛ **Program List**   Lists programs set up to run from the DOS Shell.

The active area shows up highlighted on-screen. Looking back at Figure XA.2, you can see that the Directory Tree area is active because its title bar (the part at the top) is darker than the title bars of the other areas.

To move from one area to another in the Shell, just click anywhere within that area with the mouse. Easy.

Changing Drives and Directories

The active disk drive is highlighted at the top of the screen. To display files on a different drive, click on that drive in the Drive Icons area.

The directory you select in the Directory Tree determines which files will show up in the File List area. To choose a different directory from the Directory Tree area, just click on a directory with your mouse.

If you see a plus sign in front of a directory, that means that there are some subdirectories hiding. You can make them show their faces by clicking on the plus sign with your mouse.

I'll Take This File, and This File, and This File . . .

Before you can do something to a file (for instance, copy it or delete it), you need to select it. You can select one file or lots of files; whatever you want to work on.

To select a single file, click on it. To select several files, hold down the **Ctrl** key while you click on the files, one by one, with your mouse. Then release the Ctrl key.

Standin' at the Copier, Makin' Copies

When you copy files, the original file is left where it is, and a copy is placed where you indicate. To copy files with the mouse, select them, and then hold down the **Ctrl** key. Drag the copies where you want them. (You can drag them to a drive icon in the Drive Icons area or to a directory on the Directory Tree.) When the confirmation box appears, click on the **Yes** button.

Moving Day

When you move files, the files are relocated to where you indicate. For example, you might want to move files that you seldom use into a different directory to get them out of your way.

To move files with the mouse, select them, and hold down the **Alt** key, and drag the files to their new location. You can drag them to either a different drive in the Drive Icons area or to a directory on the Directory Tree. When the confirmation box appears, click on the **Yes** button.

I've Created a Monster, Master

You can create a new directories anywhere—under the root directory, or under an existing directory. You first click on the **Directory Tree** area, and highlight the root directory (or the existing directory under which the new directory should appear).

Then, click on the File menu to open it. Click on the Create Directory command. Type the name of the new directory (up to eight characters), and click on **OK**.

Zap! That File's Outta Here!

When a file or a directory is no longer useful, you can delete it. To delete files, select them, and press the **Delete** or **Del** key. If you selected more than one file, click on **OK**, or press **Enter**. To confirm the deletion of each file, click on the **Yes** button; to skip a file, click on the **No** button.

Unlike DOS, to delete a directory using the Shell, you must delete the files in the directory first. After all the files are gone and the directory is empty, highlight it on the Directory Tree, and press **Del**. Click on the **Yes** button when you're asked for confirmation.

What's in a Name?

To rename a file or directory, select it, open the File menu, and choose the Rename command. Type the new name in the box that appears, and select **OK** or press **Enter**. A filename/directory name can consist of eight characters, followed by a period and an optional three-character extension.

Get Me Out of This Thing!

To exit the DOS Shell and return to the DOS prompt, press **F3**. If you have a mouse, open the File menu, and select the Exit command.

There! This Shell thing wasn't so difficult after all, eh?

Appendix B

The Incredibly Handy DOS Command Reference

A Guide to Entering DOS Commands

The Parts of a DOS Command

Current drive Displays the letter of the current drive, followed by a colon.

Current directory Displays the current directory path, preceded by a backslash.

DOS prompt Typically consists of a letter indicating the current drive, followed by a greater-than sign. The prompt lets you know that DOS is waiting for a command.

DOS command Tells DOS to perform some task.

Parameter The part of a command that specifies the files, directory, or drive to work with.

Switch Specifies a command's options. It's always preceded by a forward slash.

Keep these things in mind when entering DOS commands:

☞ Nothing happens until you press **Enter**.

☞ To repeat a command exactly, press **F3**. To reuse part of a command, press the right arrow key. (→)

☞ A DOS command acts upon the files within the current drive or directory unless you specify otherwise by including a file path.

☞ A *file path* consists of three parts:

The drive the file is located on, followed by a colon, as in **C:**.

A backslash (\) followed by the complete path to the file. Start with the parent directory, and then add another backslash and a subdirectory name if applicable. Complete the path with another backslash, as in **\PROJECTS\DOSBOOK**.

End the file path with the a file name or file pattern, as in **CHAP07.DOC** or **CHAP*.DOC**.

The completed path would look like this:

C:\PROJECTS\DOSBOOK\CHAP07.DOC

CD (CHDIR)

Displays or changes the active directory.

CD\[*path*]

Example: **CD\WORD**

CLS

Clears your screen.

CLS

COPY

Copies files to a directory or disk.

> COPY [*d:*][*path*][*source.ext*]
> [*d:*][*path*][*destination.ext*]
> [/Y]

Switch:

/Y	Do not prompt before overlaying existing files.

Example: **COPY C:\AUTOEXEC.BAT A:**

DBLSPACE

Accesses the DoubleSpace maintenance program, which can be used to compress a drive or a diskette, change the size of a compressed drive, or display information.

> **DBLSPACE**

DEFRAG

Optimizes a disk by reorganizing its files.

> **DEFRAG** *d:* [/U] [/S:*order*]

Switches

/U	Leave empty spaces between files
/S:*order*	Re-sort your drive in the following order:
N	File name
E	Extension
D	Date
S	Size
-	Reverse sort order

Example: **DEFRAG D: /S:-D**

DEL

Deletes files.

> **DEL [*d*:][*path*]*filename.ext* [/P]**

Switches:

/P	Asks for confirmation before deleting a file.

Example: **DEL *.* /P**

DELTREE

Deletes a directory and its subdirectories.

> **DELTREE [/Y][*d*:]*path***

Switches:

/Y	Deletes the directory tree without first prompting you to confirm.

Example: **DELTREE C:\WORD\JUNK**

DIR

Lists files in the specified directory.

> **DIR [*d*:][*path*][*filename.ext*] [/P][/W]**
>
> **[/A:*attributes*][/O:*sortorder*]**
>
> **[/S][/B][/L][/C][/CH]**

Switches:

/P	Lists files one screen at a time.
/W	Lists files across the screen.
/A	Lists files with selected attributes.

/O	Lists files in the selected order.
/S	Lists files in subdirectories too.
/B	Lists files with no heading.
/L	Lists files in lowercase.
/C	Displays disk compression information, using a default 8K cluster size.
/CH	Displays disk compression information, using the cluster size of the host computer.

Example: **DIR /P**

DISKCOPY

Copies a diskette.

   DISKCOPY *sourcedisk*: *destinationdisk*:

Example: **DISKCOPY A: A:**

DOSSHELL

Starts the DOS Shell.

   DOSSHELL

EDIT

Starts the DOS Editor and (optionally) loads a file to edit.

   EDIT [*d*:][*path*][*filename.ext*]

Example: **EDIT C:\AUTOEXEC.BAT**

FORMAT

Prepares a diskette for use.

FORMAT d: [/S][F:size][/Q][/U][/V:label][/B][/C]

Switches:

/S	Creates a bootable diskette.
/F	Formats to the specified size.
/Q	Performs a quick format.
/U	Performs an unconditional format.
/V	Adds a volume label to the formatted disk.
/B	Allocates space for system files, but does not copy them.
/C	Tests all sectors to see if they are usable.

Example: **FORMAT A: /F:360**

HELP

Accesses the DOS help system

HELP [*command*]

Example: **HELP DISKCOPY**

MD (MKDIR)

Creates a directory.

MD [*d:*] *path*

Example: **MD C:\WORD\DOCS**

MEM

Displays available memory.

MEM [/P][/C][/F]

Switches:

/P	Displays one screenful at a time.
/C	Displays the programs in memory.
/F	Lists free memory.

MEMMAKER

Runs MemMaker, a program which automatically configures your system for best memory usage.

MEMMAKER

MOVE

Moves files to the location you specify. Also used to rename directories.

**MOVE [*d:*][*oldpath*]*filename.ext*
[*d:*][*newpath*][*filename.ext*]
[/Y]**

MOVE *olddirname* *newdirname*

Switch:

/Y	Overlay existing files without prompting.

Example: **MOVE C:\OLDSUB C:\NEWSUB** or
MOVE C:\MKTG\JFSALES.DOC
D:\SALES\DSSALES.DOC

MSAV

Runs Microsoft Anti-Virus, which checks the indicated drives for existing viruses, and optionally removes them.

MSAV [*d:*] [/C] [/A] [/L] [/N]

Switches:

/C	Removes any viruses it finds.
/A	Scans all drives but A: and B:
/L	Scans only local drives, not network drives.
/N	Scans for viruses while not displaying the normal interface. Use this switch at startup.

MSBACKUP

Starts MS Backup, which you can use to back up or restore your hard disk or selected directories or files.

MSBACKUP

PROMPT

Customizes the DOS prompt.

PROMPT [$P][$G][$D][$T][*text*]

Options:

$P	Displays current directory path.
$G	Displays the greater-than sign.

$D	Displays the current date.
$T	Displays the current time.
text	Displays the indicated text.

Example: **PROMPT $P Enter your command here$G**

RD (RMDIR)

Removes a directory if it's empty of files.

RD [*d:*]*path*

Example: **RD \PROGRAMS\JUNK**

REN (RENAME)

Renames a file.

REN [*d:*][*path*]*originalname.ext* [*d:*][*path*]*newname.ext*

Example: **REN OLDFILE.DOC NEWFILE.DOC**

SCANDISK

Locates and repairs disk problems. Can optionally undo its own repairs.

SCANDISK *d:* **[/ALL][/CHECKONLY]**
[/AUTOFIX][/NOSAVE][/SURFACE]

SCANDISK /UNDO *d:*

Switches

/ALL	Scans all disks.
/CHECK ONLY	Checks for, but does not repair problems.

/AUTOFIX	Repairs problems without prompting.
/NOSAVE	Deletes, but does not save cross-linked files.
/SURFACE	Performs a surface scan.
/UNDO	Undoes the repairs made by a recent ScanDisk.

TREE

Displays directory paths.

TREE [*d*:][*path*][/F][/A] [|MORE]

Switches:

/F	Lists files in each directory.
/A	Produces an alternate character for the lines that link subdirectories. Use for printer output.
|MORE	Using the MORE filter with the TREE command will cause the output to display one screen at a time.

Example: **TREE /F |MORE**

TYPE

Displays the contents of a file.

TYPE [*d*:][*path*]*filename.ext* [|MORE]

Options:

|MORE	Using the MORE filter with the TYPE command will cause the output to display one screen at a time.

Example: **TYPE C:\AUTOEXEC.BAT |MORE**

UNDELETE

Restores deleted files. Also used to establish a delete file tracking system.

**UNDELETE [*d*:][*path*][/LIST][/DT][/DS][/DOS]
[/ALL][/PURGE]
[/LOAD][/UNLOAD][/STATUS][/S[*drive*]]
[/T[*drive*]]**

Switches:

/LIST	Lists all files that can be undeleted.
/DT	Uses the tracking file when undeleting.
/DS	Uses the delete sentry file when undeleting.
/DOS	Uses DOS when undeleting.
/ALL	Undeletes without prompting.
/PURGE	Purges the DELETE SENTRY directory.
/LOAD	Loads UNDELETE.
/UNLOAD	Unloads UNDELETE.

/STATUS	Displays status on UNDELETE.
/S	Enables delete sentry.
/T	Enables delete tracking.

Example: **UNDELETE \PROGRAMS\JUNK /LIST**

UNFORMAT

Unformats a diskette.

UNFORMAT *d*: [/P][/L][/TEST]

Switches:

/P	Sends output to printer.
/L	Lists files and directories found on disk.
/TEST	Verifies that an UNFORMAT can be done, but doesn't do it.

VER

Displays the current DOS version.

VER

VOL

Displays (and lets you change) the volume label of a disk.

VOL [*d*:]

VSAFE

Loads a memory-resident anti-virus program which detects viruses as you work.

VSAFE

Appendix C

What's New in DOS 6 and 6.2?

New DOS 6 Enhancements

If you are upgrading from a previous version of DOS, such as DOS 4, or DOS 5, here is a list of enhancements that were introduced with DOS 6. At the end of this appendix, you'll find the additional enhancements introduced with DOS 6.2.

AUTOEXEC.BAT and CONFIG.SYS

You can define several configuration files and select which one to boot with. You can bypass commands selectively in AUTOEXEC.BAT or CONFIG.SYS, or even boot your computer without them.

DELTREE

Use the DELTREE command to delete a directory and its subdirectories, without having to remove its files. See Lesson 9 for more details.

DoubleSpace

Allows you to compress a disk or diskette so that it will hold up to two times more data. Once DoubleSpace is installed, it works invisibly. See Lessons 12 and 13 for more details.

EMM386

Improvements let EMM386.EXE take better advantage of unused areas in upper memory. Programs are able to use either expanded or extended memory as needed, without changing your PC's configuration.

Help

On-line Help has been expanded to a complete, graphical, on-line reference to all commands. See Lesson 5.

Interlink

Provides the ability to link two computers (such as a laptop and a desktop computer) together to transfer files, and so on.

MemMaker

MemMaker configures your PC automatically to take best advantage of the memory you have. MemMaker moves device drivers, memory-resident programs, and even DOS out of conventional memory, providing more working memory for all of your programs. See Lesson 18 for more details.

MEM

MEM provides more details about your system's memory usage. Using the /P switch causes MEM to display information one screen at a time. See Lesson 18 for more details.

Microsoft Anti-Virus

DOS now comes with a complete and easy-to-use program for virus detection and removal, based on Central Point's Anti-Virus. There is also an Anti-Virus for Windows. See Lesson 17 for more details.

Microsoft Defragmenter

Based on the Norton Utilities, the Defragmenter can reorganize the files on your PC to allow for faster disk access. See Lesson 14.

Microsoft Mail

Provides ability to send and receive electronic mail (E-mail).

MOVE

Move files and rename directories with this versatile command. See Lessons 7 and 9 for more information.

MSBACKUP

Replacing DOS's antiquated BACKUP program is MSBACKUP, a graphical backup and restore program based on Norton Backup. See Lesson 15 for more details. A version of MSBACKUP is also provided for Windows.

POWER

Makes better use of your laptop's power.

SmartDrive

Improvements in writing and reading information lets SmartDrive make best use of system resources.

UNDELETE

Provides better tracking and easier recovery of deleted files. There is now an UNDELETE for Windows. See Lesson 8 for more details.

Workgroup Connection

Provides the ability to use shared directories and printers.

New DOS 6.2 Enhancements

In this section you'll find a listing of the additional enhancements introduced with DOS 6.2.

DoubleGuard

Verifies data being written from memory to a DoubleSpace drive, protecting against data corruption caused by errant programs. See Lesson 12.

DoubleSpace Enhancements

Besides DoubleGuard, DoubleSpace now performs a surface scan on each disk before double-spacing it. This ensures the integrity of the compressed data. You can now uncompress a compressed drive, if you want. In addition, compressed diskettes are now mounted automatically. See Lessons 12 and 13.

SmartDrive Enhancements

SmartDrive performs primarily read-caching. Write-caching is turned off by default. Caching of CD-ROMs is now supported.

ScanDisk

ScanDisk replaces the old command, CHKDSK, scanning disks and performing repairs. ScanDisk works on double-spaced drives, in addition to noncompressed drives.

ScanDisk repairs more damage than the old CHKDSK command. For example, cross-linked files can be accurately detected and repaired. In addition,

ScanDisk can perform surface testing on a disk.

Multiple Configurations in AUTOEXEC.BAT

Similar to the multiple configuration enhancement for CONFIG.SYS that was released in DOS 6.0, DOS 6.2 now supports the same thing in the AUTOEXEC.BAT. It's not really as complex as it sounds, but check with your manual if you want more specific information.

Other Enhancements

DOS 6.2 introduces many subtle but nice enhancements, such as:

- ☛ **Faster DISKCOPY**   DISKCOPY now uses the hard disk to temporarily store data that speeds the copy process and reduces disk swapping.

- ☛ **Copy protection**   COPY, MOVE, and XCOPY now prompt the user before copying a file over an existing version.

- ☛ **A comment on commas**   Commands which typically display large numbers, such as DIR, FORMAT, and MEM, now display those numbers with commas as in 1,023,476.

- ☛ **Goodbye, Shell!**   The DOS Shell is not included with DOS 6.2, but if you're upgrading from a previous version of DOS, it still exists. Simply copy it to the \DOS from the \OLD_DOS.1 subdirectory created by Setup.

Appendix D

Installing DOS

Before you start dilly-dallying around, have a formatted diskette (for drive A) ready. It will be used to create an Uninstall diskette, which can be used to return to your previous DOS version if you encounter problems. (If you are using double-density diskettes, have two diskettes ready.)

To install DOS 6.2 on your system, first place the Setup diskette in its drive. Then, type either **A:** or **B:** (depending upon which drive the disk is in), and press **Enter**. Type **SETUP** and press **Enter**.

From here on out, just follow the on-screen instructions. When requested, place one of the formatted diskettes in drive A, and the Uninstall diskette will be created. Put this diskette in a safe place. (If you want to uninstall DOS 6.2 at some later time, place this diskette in drive A and reboot.)

Swap the disks when prompted. After all the DOS 6.2 files have been copied, remove the final setup diskette, and press **Enter**. Your system will reboot under DOS 6.2—and you're ready to go!

Index

Symbols

* (asterisk) wild card
  listing files, 32
  specifying files, 20
/ (forward slash), switches, 15
/? switch, 23
> (greater-than sign) redirection
  symbol, 33
? (question mark) wild card
  listing files, 32
  specifying files, 20
\ (backslash), root directory, 11
|MORE parameter, 45

A

Access Denied message, 41
/ALL switch, SCANDISK
  command, 54
Anti-Virus (Microsoft),
  83-86, 117
archiving files, 40
asterisk (*) wild card
  listing files, 32
  specifying files, 20
AUTOEXEC.BAT file, 4-6
  DOS 6 enhancements, 116
  modifying, 93-95
  multiple configurations, 120
/AUTOFIX switch, SCANDISK
  command, 54
automatic virus scans, 85-86

B

backslash (\), root directory, 11
Backspace key, 16

backup catalogs, 73
Backup dialog box, 74-76
backups, 72-73
  archiving files, 40
  diskettes, 51-53
  full, 74-75
  incremental and
    differential, 75
  restoring, 78-80
  specific directories or files,
    76-77
Bad command or file name
  message, 46, 96
batch files, 5
blank lines, inserting, 95
bootable diskettes
  creating, 48-49
  virus-safe, 83
booting PCs (personal
  computers), 1-3
bytes, 29, 88

C

/C switch, DIR command, 65-66
canceling commands in
  progress, 16
CD (CHDIR) command,
  12-13, 104
chains, lost, 53-55
characters in file names, 10
/CHECKONLY switch,
  SCANDISK command, 54
CHKDSK command, 53
cleaning viruses from system,
  83, 85
clicking, 25, 98
CLS command, 104
clusters, lost, 53-55

Other Idiot-Proof Books from Alpha!

If you enjoyed this Complete Idiot's Pocket Guide, then you may want to check out the rest!

Complete Idiot's Pocket Guides

The Complete Idiot's
Pocket Guide to DOS 6
ISBN: 1-56761-303-9
Softbound, $5.99 USA

The Complete Idiot's
Pocket Guide to Windows
(version 3.1)
ISBN: 1-56761-302-0
Softbound, $5.99 USA

The Complete Idiot's
Pocket Guide to
WordPerfect for Windows
(version 6.0)
ISBN: 1-56761-371-3
Softbound, $5.99 USA

The Complete Idiot's
Pocket Guide to
WordPerfect 6
ISBN: 1-56761-300-4
Softbound, $5.99 USA

The Complete Idiot's
Pocket Guide to Word for
Windows (version 2)
ISBN: 1-56761-301-2
Softbound, $5.99 USA

Tip

If you can't find these books at your local computer book retailer, call this toll-free number for more information! 1-800-428-5331